Punk Rock

A Visual Biography

Punk Rock

A Visual Biography

WYMER
PUBLISHING
Bedford, England

First published in Great Britain in 2023
by Wymer Publishing
www.wymerpublishing.co.uk
Tel: 01234 326691
Wymer Publishing is a trading name of Wymer (UK) Ltd

This edition copyright © 2023 Wymer Publishing.

ISBN: 978-1-915246-23-3

The Author hereby asserts his rights to be identified
as the author of this work in accordance with sections
77 to 78 of the Copyright, Designs & Patents Act 1988.

All rights reserved. No part of this publication may be
reproduced or transmitted in any form or by any means,
electronic or mechanical, including photocopying, or any
information storage and retrieval system, without written
permission from the publisher.

This publication is sold subject to the condition that it shall not,
by way of trade or otherwise, be lent, re-sold, hired out or
otherwise circulated without the publishers prior consent in any
form of binding or cover other than that in which it is published
and without a similar condition including this condition
being imposed on the subsequent purchaser.

Every effort has been made to trace the copyright holders of the
photographs in this book but some were unreachable. We would
be grateful if the photographers concerned would contact us.

Design by Andy Bishop/1016 Sarpsborg
Printed and bound by Halstan, Amersham, Buckinghamshire.

A catalogue record for this book is available from the British Library.

Roll Of Honour

Wymer Publishing duly acknowledges the following people who all put their faith in this publication by pre-ordering it:

Suzanne Airey
Stephen Allan
Stewart Apperley
Tracey Armstrong
Darren Ball
Richard Bannister
Robin Barker
Sharon Barlow
David Billingsley
Roy Bird
Steven Bland
Graham Brierley
Nancy Briggs
Graham Brown
Mike Burchell
Boyd Campbell
Steve Carroll
Colin Cartwright
Brian Clark
Kevin Collins
Chris Cook
Adrian Cooper
Richard Cope
Rob Cork
Mark Corpus-Seventy Seven
Helen Crawford
James Cummings
Stewart Currie
Simon Curtis
Clare Dallimore
Peter Davidson
Keith Dingwall
Jessica Dixon
Louise Dobson
Chris Doyle
Deborah Drummond
Alan Dymonds
Alexander Edwards
Jacquie Elliott
Steve Falconer
David Forrester
Steve Frain
Teresa Gale
Sandra Gibbs

Sean Gillen
Stephen Greaves
Craig Griffiths
David Harper
Mike Harrell
Simon Hemingway
Lynn Hending
Sandra Henwood
Jonathan Hill
Abbie Holder
Alan Hopkinson
Brian Hopper
Nick Humphreys
Jo-ann Jackson
Kevin Jarvis
Alexis Jones
Wendy Kaye
Simon Kealey
Alison Keating
Kevin Knott
Stephen Lambert
Hazel Laming
Clare Lawrie
Ian Lees
Pauline Lockwood
Richard Lomas
Stephen Longford
Carly Lovell
Alan Low
Paula Mackley
Alan Marie
Paul Martin
Dave Massey
Gary McCrindle
June Miller
David Moore
Hazel Morgan
Owen Munro
Tim Murden
Steve Murphy
Trevor Norton
Eileen Oldfield
Lee Oliver
Julie Payne

Paul Pearson
Jason Pegler
Steven Pitcher
Patrick Pitt
Mark Potts
Pete Procter
Christopher Ramsay
Carrie Rankin
Steve Redman
Julie Reid
Keith Roberts
Clive Robinson
Samantha Rose
Peter Rudkin
Chris Rye
Pete Sadler
James Satchwell
Paul Savage
Sue Scully
Tim Shaw
Lester Sherwood
Gary Shields
Gavin Short
Robert Sloss
Brendan Smith
Lindsey Smith
Derek Strong
Lorraine Taylor
Celia Taylor
Deb Thomas
Paul Tunstall
Robby Wade
Gwyneth Wakeham
Stephen Webb
Graham Whitelaw
David Whitmore
Andy Williams
Jules Williamson
Nicola Winter
Martin Wisbey
Matt Wood
Michelle Young
Laurie Young

Clean it up! Pistols get EMI ultimatum

By Michael Kilbane

PUNK ROCK group Sex Pistols were warned today by the EMI recording company to tone down their behaviour or risk losing a £40,000 two-year recording contract.

Sir John Read, chairman of EMI Limited, whose subsidiary has had the four-letter group under contract since October, said cancellation of the contract 'is something we shall certainly have to consider" if the group did not alter its way.

Sir John gave the group a week to improve. He was speaking after delivering a public warning to the group in front of 150 shareholders at the annual general meeting of EMI Limited in London today.

Sir John said the group's records " were acceptable and they have behaved perfectly satisfactorily in respect of their recording contract." The contract didn't cover TV or personal appearances.

"But we might have to consider breaking their contract" if the group did not change their attitude, he said.

The public resented the group's behaviour, he added. They were "hurting themselves and their record sales. It is very foolish of them."

"Certainly we would be breaching the contract if we cancelled it. We would be liable." But public duty was more important, he said, than any financial or legal considerations.

In a statement to the meeting which was seen as a move to defuse the explosive situation around the group following their four-letter outburst on the Today television programme last Wednesday, Sir John said: "I need hardly add that we shall do everything we can to restrain their public behaviour although this is a matter over which we have no real control."

Sir John said after the meeting that the group's insult to the Queen at last night's Leeds concert made it only worse for them when the contract situation was being reviewed.

Bemused

Sir John was referring to the Pistol's show at Leeds Polytechnic last night, the first since last week's four-letter furore.

The group's promise to cut out drinking and swearing disintegrated within minutes and some students walked out claiming the music was "rubbish."

Before the show started local students' union leader Ian Steele was told by the tour manager that the group had cleaned up their act.

But as soon as the Sex Pistols hit the stage it was obvious they were determined to live up to their crude and belligerent image.

'The first number is dedicated to Bill Grundy and the Queen. It goes—F - - Ya," began singer Johnny Rotten

"I hope you have a really bad night. I hate you all," he leered before the band spluttered into their first bout of violent hard rock.

For a number of students Rotten's sentiments rang too true, for several appeared bemused and disappointed by the whole affair.

One said : " It is the worst group I have ever heard. They did not shock me. Their music was just so bad."

The latest theatre to cancel a Sex Pistols show is the new 1500-seat Roxy at Harlesden. The group were to have marked the theatre's opening with two Christmas concerts.

Pistols' no aggro pledge for City concert

PUNK Rock band Sex Pistols—at the centre of a television "dirty words" row —are due to appear at the Liverpool Stadium next Saturday.

Yesterday, as seven bookings for the band's nationwide tour were called off, their leader, Johnny Rotten, pledged No trouble.

But the Rev Donald Gray, Rector of Liverpool, said he was worried about the band's Merseyside visit.

'Anarchy doesn't give freedoms, it takes them away," he said.

Cancelled concerts are at Newcastle, Bournemouth, Lancaster, Preston, Bristol, Birmingham and, last night University of East Anglia, Norwich.

Tonight, before a booking in Derby, Sex Pistols will have to give a private audition to councillors, council officials and pressmen

SEX PISTOLS, the punk rock band who caused a public uproar on TV. The band comprises: In front—Steve Jones, left, and Johnny Rotten. At rear Glen Matlock, left, and Paul Cook.

what was said during fifteen minutes.

EVENING STANDARD, THURSDAY, DECEMBER 1, 1976—3

'Worthless, decidedly inferior, displeasing...'
The Punks— Rotten and proud of it!

PUNK STYLE—Sex Pistols Johnny Rotten (left) and Steve Jones in action recently at Notre Dame Hall, Leicester Square.

NEWS ON CAMERA

"*PUNK — Worthless, decidedly inferior, displeasing, rotten.*"
—Partridge's Dictionary of Slang and Unconventional English.

PUNK ROCK, which exploded on to the TV screen last night in a string of four-letter words, is a bizarre movement which combines rock and rebellion, writes **James Johnson**.

It is almost a social rather than a musical phenomenon. Its leading exponents, including the Sex Pistols, possess no great musical expertise.

The attractions for their followers are their youth, their energy and their tendencies towards boorish arrogance. The movement already has its own record shops and magazines, and a notorious Punk paper called Sniffin' Glue, which is run by an unemployed Deptford youth who is known simply as Mark P.

Punk Rockers pick bizarre names. The Sex Pistols' lead singer calls himself Johnny Rotten. Another leading group, The Damned, include Captain Sensible and Rat Scabies in their line-up. A famous fan is Sid the Vicious.

The Sex Pistols claim they are striking a blow against the superstar rock establishment, who, they say, have grown out of touch with the so-called "blank generation," the 1976 breed of youth brought up on frustration and unemployment.

But their protest is also a sound commercial proposition. The Sex Pistols are under contract to EMI and their first record was released this week. The title—Anarchy in the UK.

Over the last six months, the group has been banned from appearing at various London rock venues, including the Nashville, the Kensington, the 100 Club in Oxford Street—where the Punk boom started—and Dingwalls.

Today they were busy rehearsing for a country-wide tour. They open at University of East Anglia, Norwich, tomorrow and the tour, which includes bookings in Dundee Glasgow and the West Country, will continue until Boxing Day.

Joining them are three other Punk groups, the Damned, the Clash and from America, Johnny Thunder's Heartbreakers.

Their record say EMI, is selling healthily."

Of the row over their TV appearance, an EMI spokesman said: "We regret that the media have resorted to such sensationalism. In no way has our relationship with the group been affected."

SEX PISTOLS unrepentant — guitarist Steve Jones (left) and drummer Dave Cook in Oxford Street on their way to a rehearsal today.

Southern Weekend Journeys

There will be delays on some Southern Region main lines this weekend, particularly on Sunday, while engineers carry out track maintenance and bridge reconstruction between stations on the following routes:

LONDON to KENT COAST
between Deal and Minster
between Charing Cross and London Bridge (see panel below)

LONDON to SUSSEX COAST
between Hassocks and Brighton
between Battle and West St. Leonards
between Ford and Chichester
between Lewes and Berwick
between Charing Cross and London Bridge (see panel below)

LONDON to MAIDSTONE EAST
between Maidstone East and Lenham

LONDON to PORTSMOUTH
between Ford and Chichester also at Woking station

LONDON to GATWICK AIRPORT at Victoria station

Suburban services will also be delayed between
Charing Cross and London Bridge — Ascot and Wokingham
Victoria and Sydenham Hill — South Croydon and Coulsdon
also at Victoria station

There will be no services from Waterloo (South Eastern) and Charing Cross this weekend. During this period, all services will be diverted to Cannon Street with the exception of Caterham/Tattenham Corner services which will run to and from London Bridge. There will be a train shuttle service between Charing Cross/Waterloo and Cannon Street.

For details of service alterations and delays please ring 01-928 5100

kids who use ordinary uage."

THE SEX PISTOLS AT THE PARADISO CLUB, AMSTERDAM, 1977

'See ya at the end of the world...'

Punk funk: Call it Rotten roll...

"ANARCHY, anarchy, anarchy," screams a malevolent singer called Johnny Rotten.

"See ya at the end of the world," he declares as his group the Sex Pistols launch into an extra high-volume slice of rock music and the crowd at the foot of the stage succumb to a glazed kind of frenzy.

The scene is a hot, crowded club in Oxford Street which for one night a week has lately become the centre for a style of music loosely known as punk-rock.

Human

With a repertoire that includes such numbers as I'm Pretty Vacant, I'm In Love With Myself and Anarchy In The UK, the Sex Pistols—all less than 20—have become the leaders of the field.

Admirers claim they represent a blow against the superior attitude of established superstars and that their music represents a move back to rebellion and aggression. Equally, it is said, they are an expression of the frustration and nihilism that is current among many young people.

"You can talk to the Pistols as people," says one follower Claudio Maguani, 18. "They're human. If you go and see the Rolling Stones you're hardly likely to bump into Mick Jagger in the toilet."

Apart from Johnny Rotten, the group consists of Glen

FAITHFUL FOLLOWER.— Claudio Maguani and friend.

Matlock (bass), Paul Cook (drums) and Steve Jones (guitar). The only roots they will reveal is that they come from "the wrong end of London."

Punks and punk rockers alike appear to place great emphasis on being against almost everything except themselves. The establishment, hippies and intellectuals are all equally despised.

Bizarre

With typical antagonism singer Johnny Rotten refuses to do interviews with the Press. When approached he responds with a terse "F... off."

Not unnaturally, therefore, it all adds up to bizarre night out whenever the Sex Pistols appear. Earlier this week they topped the bill over other punk rock groups like the Buzzcocks and Vibratos at the 100 Club, Oxford Street, and while Rotten went through lyrics like I'm so pretty, we're so pretty and we don't care," their most extreme followers went through the motions of something close to a fashion show.

Just as a certain harsh dogmatic attitude pervades the punk rock scene the participants dress in post-Bowie styles that revolve around dyed hair, immaculately torn tee-shirts, leather trousers and chains.

Anne Ferris a 16 year old with hair dyed blue, said: " My mother is not shocked by anything I do now. When I dyed my hair she just accepted it as another new style."

Meanwhile the group and their followers have recently been attracting a great deal of interest from the music Press and Britain's leading record companies.

Less partisan observers are unsure whether it adds up to a new cultural phenomenon or just a giant confidence trick.

But if the Pistols have their way by this time next year Britain's teenagers will be singing along with Anarchy In The UK.

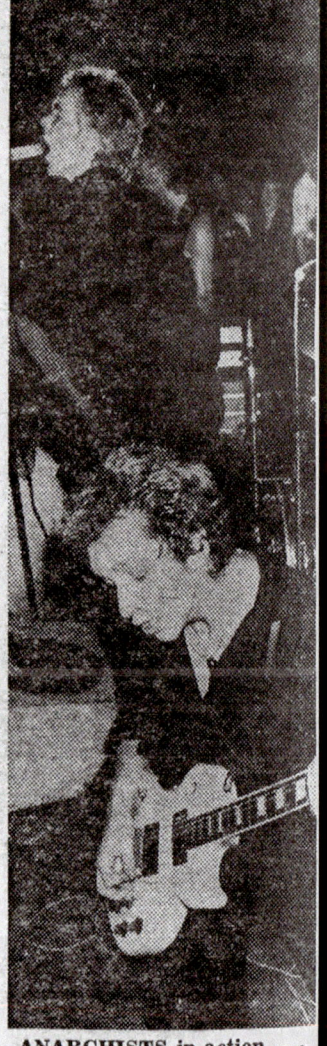

ANARCHISTS in action... the Sex Pistols on stage. "We're so pretty and we don't care."

SOUNDS!

It's Junk Rock!

DAVID GRITTEN meets the self-styled king of hate

THEY HAVE been called the Blank Generation.

They are the teenage kids who follow "punk rock" — the new wave in rock music.

Punk group the Sex Pistols, who used obscene language on a TV programme, have now been banned from Birmingham Town Hall, and other halls.

Punk Rock music is bad enough — monotonous, loud, and incompetent.

But its followers are worse.

They have adopted the most alarming fashions, all for the sake of calculated outrage.

Boys wear their hair short, spiky and scruffy. They wear ripped T-shirts, or occasionally make tops from plastic dustbin liners.

They sport safety pins or chains, worn through the ear lobes, the nose, or even the inside of the mouth.

Girls go for black lipstick, lurid make-up with stars painted round their eyes, and fetishist clothes in rubber or cire.

Punk Rock disciples (and some of its exponents) daub themselves with swastikas and make approving comments about Fascism and violence.

They don't want to know the views or the attitudes of anyone in authority or anyone over the age of 21.

Hate Jagger

Punk rockers hate rich, established pop stars like Rod Stewart, Mick Jagger and Elton John ferociously.

Violence has broken out at clubs where Punk Rock is played. One boy had part of an ear bitten off, a girl was blinded in one eye by flying glass.

Self-appointed king of Punk Rock is a 20-year-old who rejoices in the name of Johnny Rotten. He is lead singer of the Sex Pistols.

Such is the commercial interest in the Sex Pistols that EMI paid them a reputed £40,000 advance to sign them up.

They have their first single released this week. It is called "Anarchy In The UK."

I talked to Rotten this week in what could be described as difficult circumstances. He belched, swore and was frequently abusive.

"Yes, we're leaders of a movement. The Sex Pistols were the first, but other groups are following us.

"We all want to put some honesty and guts back into music.

"I hate the Jaggers and the Stewarts. They are so hypocritical. They are just lining their own pockets. They sing songs about love — stupid songs — but they don't mean it.

"There's no such thing as love, anyway.

"But I just don't regard them at all; they are redundant, clapped out."

Trap

But might not Rotten turn out the same if he became rich and famous?

"Trying to trap me, are you?" he sneers. "The answer is no — because the Sex Pistols come from working class backgrounds. We don't care about money — we just don't think of it.

"Might be not feel different about it as he got older?

"Look," he says, "how old are you?"

"I'm 22," I say.

"Oh. Well, you're just completely irrelevant, then, aren't you?"

Try another tack. Was he not worried about the violent image of punk-rock?

"Another trap. Well, you see, it's just the Press and everyone trying to stir up trouble because of just a couple of incidents.

"We don't encourage violence — all we say is, if there is something in your way, you don't lie back and let it tread all over you, you do something about it.

"All that peace and love rubbish — that was just the hypocrisy of that other generation — the one we hate."

What were Sex Pistols songs about, then?

"Real things, honest things. About the numb feeling of living on a council estate, the boredom of a nine-to-five job, about suburbia and having 2.4 children. We're down to earth, we haven't got our head in the clouds like those others."

Personally, the Pistols worry me. Their music, judging from "Anarchy In The UK" is just mish-mash.

In my view, fans who care about rock should stay away from the Pistols and their like. They make no worthwhile contribution to music.

SID VICIOUS IN HAMBURG

The Rolling Stones are Establishment to young Punk followers. STEVE TURNER reports

The anarchic rock of the young and doleful

Johnny Rotten and Sex Pistols: could replace Jagger as a symbol

AND THEN THERE was punk. Tonight the Sex Pistols, focal point of the newly dubbed punk generation, take off on their first concert tour of Britain complete with a £40,000 contract with EMI Records, a single entitled Anarchy In The UK, and a reputation for being insolent and violent—a reputation which was compounded through their use of Thames Television's Today programme to throw out a few live obscenities which would appal the parents and therefore thrill the kids.

In a business in which shock means press coverage and press coverage means free advertising the Sex Pistols are quite clearly on their way to national fame. After too many years of drug-taking, peace-loving, long-haired gentlemen what better news value than drug-hating, hate-loving, short-haired gentlemen who, as Bill Grundy said on Today "make the Rolling Stones seem clean?"

To visit a Sex Pistols performance is to look in on an expanding new youth culture that has no time for drugs and long hair, frowns on flared jeans, thinks the Rolling Stones are establishment, and has outright contempt for philosophies of love and peace. Most of the young punks are between 17 and 19. To be in your twenties is to be old. They've all grown up with a music that they felt alienated from—groups too old to identify with, musicianship too sophisticated to ape, concerts too expensive to attend, and songs that were no reflection of their feelings or problems. The lives of the stars were becoming increasingly separate from their own with the Rod Stewarts of rock escaping to Los Angeles to relieve their tax suffering while they themselves left school to join the dole queue.

The music they naturally latched on to and then created themselves is raw and unsophisticated, as easy to learn as skiffle, with lyrics that had something to do with living in Harlesden or Bromley, with being unemployed, or with the Notting Hill riots. Only three of the bands (The Damned, the Sex Pistols, and the Vibrators) have recording contracts: mostly the prime object is to perform.

Punks are from the generation to whom pornography is just another comic book. They were 9 or 10 when Penthouse first went pubic. They picked up on fashions portrayed in Club International and Forum which were sold at King's Road boutique called Sex (now renamed "seditionaries") run by the Sex Pistols' manager, a 28-year-old called Malcolm McLaren. They came out with leather tee-shirts, swastika armbands, bondage outfits and a variety of rubber-wear and tee-shirts designed to shock. One of the boutiques' best-sellers is a shirt portraying the Cambridge rapist. Another, featuring two homosexual cowboys, caused an arrest last year.

Johnny Rotten, lead singer with the Sex Pistols, reflects this new jaded attitude to sex by saying that he's not exactly against it but that it's all been done between twelve and twenty. Love, he says, is something that people feel for animals; it doesn't apply to humans. Lust is what happens between humans.

The favourite films of the punks are The Texas Chain Saw Massacre and Death Weekend. The most influential oldie is Clockwork Orange, and some have even taken to pencilling in the single eyelash, Alex style.

Like the Mods of the early sixties the punks emanate from suburban London with contingents in places as far away as Nottingham, Durham, and Manchester. They're mostly working-class and mostly unemployed. The Sex Pistols themselves come from Shepherds Bush, birthplace of The Who, and have only been performing for 12 months. Their songs, which deal with anarchy, apathy, and violence, are written by Johnny Rotten, who was chosen for the group by McLaren after he turned up at Sex and displayed his talents by miming to the juke box. Rotten is 20, has pallid insolent looks that could replace Jagger's lips as a symbol of youthful arrogance, and smears Nivea Cream in his short hair to make it stick up. He and the Pistols are preparing a song called There's No Future, to the tune of the national anthem.

The punks in short have been told by their elders that morals are a matter for the individual to decide upon, and they've taken the message to heart. Hippies used to proudly emblazon walls with the statement, "We are the children our parents warned us against." Punks might well scrawl, "We are the children the Festival of Light warned us against."

THE OBSERVER, SUNDAY 5 DECEMBER 1976

How punk became a four-letter word

by JEREMY BUGLER

Punk group The Damned: The next generation?

TONY Mc

MALCOLM McLAREN, young manager of the Sex Pistols rock group, munched at a sausage sandwich in a North London cafe, cleared his throat and delivered: 'Punk Rock players are nearly all ex-Borstal or unemployed lads. They are England's next generation and we will learn to be proud of them.'

At a neighbouring table a little earlier, four punk rock musicians had drunk tea out of glass cups. Their hair was short-cropped, sometimes almost shaved, sometimes dyed a vivid Belisha Beacon orange. Safety pins, old bicycle chains, razor blades served as jewellery. Clothes were torn or odd: drainpipe lurex trousers were favoured. Teeth seemed a little green.

The fear that the punk rock people might just conceivably turn out to be England's next generation last week dramatically revived the British capacity for indignation. Alliterative headlines in the popular prints ('The Filth and the Fury' — *Daily Mirror*), cancellations of concert engagements, a strike by EMI staff dispatching copies of the Sex Pistol's new record from the factory have launched the cult of punk rock from obscurity to notoriety in the time it took to shock Thames Television viewers with a string of four-letter words.

Punk rock has arrived so quickly that there's not even broad agreement about what to call it. 'High energy rock' say the Sex Pistols. 'New Wave rock' say the Damned. 'Dole Queue rock' says one critic. 'Nasty Kid rock,' says another.

But all are agreed that punk-rock is played almost exclusively by working-class kids, has come from nothing in the last 12 months, arriving at a small-scale festival in London in September, and is doing its job by inflaming the good, the decent and the hard-working. Punk rock bands are undoubtedly bursting out all over Britain—in Manchester, where the Buzzcocks and a group called Slaughter and the Dogs are busy, in Birmingham, Cardiff and London.

They also agree that punk-rock musicians have a lot in *common*: outside *music*, they'd be dead-end kids. Malcolm McLaren, an articulate ex-art student, said: 'They are part of this generation which has come out of school with no future, no jobs, no chance to buy decent clothes because they have no money, and only a lot of unemployment ahead of them.'

The punk rock musicians produced their pedigree. Johnny Rotten of the Pistols: 'Unemployed and bored to death.' David Vanium of the Damned: 'I had a job as a gravedigger for a year.' Two other Damned musicians (Rat Scabies and Captain Sensible—baptismal names are lost for ever) met while employed as lavatory attendants at the Fairfield Halls, Croydon.

In contrast to the public rage, experienced observers of rock music are by no means willing to write off punk rock. John Peel's been nice and Charles Shaar Murray, a respected critic on the *New Musical Express*, said that punk rock can be understood only by seeing what's gone before and what's around.

The context, he said, is first of all roots in 'the acne and garage-band rock' of the late sixties in America. (The Damned actually have a song called 'Picking Spots.') The drive, then and now, is 'a dissatisfaction with the rock-bands of the sixties, still with us, which seems to have *got old*, rich, self-obsessed and intent mainly on being tax-exiles.

'Now there's a natural desire for kids to see their contemporaries on the stage. They don't want to see rich men like The Who or the Rolling Stones.'

Contemporary commercial music can't satisfy the audience, said McLaren of the Pistols. He and others argued that the highly complex big bands, with their synthesisers and mounds of equipment, were beyond the pockets and the range of the typical teenager. EMI seem to agree, by signing up the Pistols for £40,000 as 'a return to the basics of rock.'

McLaren added: 'This is music of the streets. The kids want something new and they don't mean an organ recital at the Wigmore Hall.' He said of the Rolling Stones: 'They're not rock. They're cabaret music.'

Mixed into the brew is a little political seasoning. 'The kids are coming out of the working class and the commercial music isn't able to express their feelings. It's the class war; I mean, you've got a whole front line here. They're political; they want to destroy the society and start again.'

Punk rock lyrics certainly go along with the business of terrifying the bourgeois. The Clash band have a song that goes: 'In 1977/There's knives in West Eleven/It ain't so lucky to be rich/'Cos there's Guns in Knightsbridge.'

The Pistols, ever anxious to be prime punks, have a new song that might well cause another stoppage at the EMI factory: 'God Save the Queen/ God Save the Fascist Regime/ It made you morons/ Into human H-bombs.'

Conversation with the punk-men, however, gives the lie to any desperate enterprise. After holding the door open, nicely, Glen Matlock, 20-year-old Pistol guitarist, said, 'Yes, you've-got-to-destroy-in-order-to-create.' 'You want revolution then?' 'Yea.' 'What kind of new society?' 'Dunno about it.' 'Socialism?'

'Socialism?' said Steve Jones, lead guitar. 'Oh, all these long words bother my head.' Johnny Rotten, the singer and perhaps the star, seemed not so much concerned with politics as with affirming that if success does come, it will not change him. 'We won't compromise.' In the meantime, the nihilist politics are part of the style, together with safety pins.

If they are asked, the Pistols and the Damned will also make broad statements about violence. These are usually nasty, though the Damned's manager, a very pleasant man called Rick Rogers, is trying to cool the vague talk.

Charles Shaar Murray, the rock critic, said: 'The Pistols are very nice boys, though they won't thank me for saying so. They've got their thumbs on the Evil button as hard as they can, but really, they're as tame as kittens.'

Murray won't go along at all with last week's sudden crop of people able to say punk rock is terrible music. The music has ben described fairly neutrally: 'Steel-hammer drums, bass guitar which combines booming intensity with melody and simplicity, lead guitar like a jagged knife and a singer whose ambition to be a star is great enough to carry them all forward.' Murray says of the Pistols: 'They're a good rock band and in two or three years they could be a great rock band.'

Not everyone is choleric about punk rock. Laurie Taylor, Professor of Sociology at York University, said: 'Rock music cults always start off with something outrageous. But in a very short time they become refined and acceptable. David Bowie's Glam Rock cult, of which these kids are the heirs, started the same way. So did the Rolling Stones.'

Memories of past outbursts about past rock groups are quoted by protectors of punk rock. They recall the days when *Encounter* published a serious treatise against Elvis Presley and television cameras would not show his lower limbs when he sang, the days when the Rolling Stones apitomised dangerous, degenerate youth.

As one man said: 'In a decade or so, we'll be hearing the Sex Pistols on "These You Have Loved".'

RAW ROCKERS SET FOR CELLAR BAR

YOU may never have heard of London rock, but when you get to know it you will see two names written right the way through it — Jive-Bombers and The Stranglers.

These two groups will be appearing at South Hill Park in the next two weeks, helping to make Rock in the Cellar Bar one of the most entertaining Sunday nights out in the area.

The Jive-Bombers have an impressive rock pedigree. The line-up includes Martin Stone on guitar (ex-Chilli Willi and the Red Hot Peppers), Wilgar Campbell on drums (ex-Rory Gallagher).

Jonah Lewis at the keyboards (ex-Terry Dactyl and the Dinosaurs and composer of their hit "Seaside Shuffle"), Thump on bass (ex-John Drummer band), and the amazing Jo-Anne Kelly guesting on vocals.

The Stranglers defy description because of their sheer variety. They are somewhere between the Doors and Velvet Underground and they recently caused a storm as support band on the recent Country Joe European tour.

Melody Maker described them as "Long, and loud, raw, rancid and riotous."

Jive-Bombers are on April 18 and Stranglers on May 9.

JOHNNY ROTTEN (they give themselves names like that, and Rat Scabies) said in a BBC interview that he had launched himself to stardom by walking up and down King's-road in Chelsea spitting at people.

"I did it because they were stupid." And the group have a new song in the pipe-line: "God Save the Queen/God Save the Fascist regime/It made you morons/Into human H bombs."

Without a doubt they have found national notoriety. They have a £40,000 contract with EMI Records, bookings for a concert tour of Britain and a reputation as the champions of the deprived young against the complacent middle-aged.

And also without question they have achieved their object of shocking the decent and the hardworking. The lines to the Thames Television studio were jammed with complaints after the programme.

Many sociologists and welfare workers are not surprised that the teeming cities have spawned rebels. They leave school, it is said, with no jobs, little money and only a lot of unemployment ahead of them.

The easiest money is in pop music, and there is a vast oil well of it in the media, where producers are not adverse to creating confrontations and one of the easiest ways is to appal parents and therefore thrill their children.

★ ★ ★

Page 16, The Advertiser, December 16, 1976

YOUTH SCENE

PISTOLS UNDER FIRE

Mike McCormack tracks down the "punk" group who shocked viewers

With Cathy Jowett

THEY sought them here, they sought them there... the Sex Pistols that is — at present the enfants terribles of the pop world.

Last week was a very good/bad (depending on your point of view) week for the Sex Pistols. A mere month ago, they were little more than just another up and coming "punk" rock band, with about 14 self composed numbers and a minor reputation on the London circuit for calculated outrage. And then, in the words of one music paper we had "The Hundred Seconds That Punk Rocked Fleet Street."

Yes, that's how long it took the band to send 'Today" presenter Bill Grundy packing to his home in Marple Bridge to contemplate what had gone wrong.

Four letter words of every Anglo-Saxon description appeared on the Thames television screen at peak viewing time as Grundy attempted to "interview" the Pistols as an example of modern youth gone mad. They didn't disappoint him or their fans. Phone calls blocked the lines at Thames and the Pistols nationwide tour was effectively wrecked as dates were cancelled and hotels decided that their "respectable" image couldn't take the notoriety.

For the national press, they were, of course, merely this month's Genesis P. Orridge, and obviously considered them to have as much to do with good music as our friend Genesis has to do with art. For myself I was interested — it's always good to be at the centre of a volcano when it erupts and I wanted to get the band's views on the whole fracas from a rock writer's point of view.

The Sex Pistols at play.

So the Advertiser joined in the hunt to track down the four intrepid 19 year olds as hotel by hotel threw them on the streets for crimes too shocking to mention. The scene is Thursday afternoon at Piccadilly Radio's foyer. With the band led of course by Johnny Rotten is their young articulate manager—Svengali figure Mr Malcolm MacLaren.

Here's a brief extract from what was said during those fifteen minutes.

MIKE: "Hi, which one's Ringo? (slight titters but not from the band) . . . just a joke. No, but what about all this fuss over the Grundy interview?"

SEX PISTOL: "Well, it's ridiculous. But we'll go along with all of this publicity It's just a laugh."

MACLAREN: "All that happened was that a bit of authentic life came onto the T.V. screens, and the chiefs didn't like it. They're just ordinary kids who use ordinary language."

MIKE: "Don't you think there's a danger that all this sort of publicity and attention you're receiving at the moment will backfire on you?"

SEX PISTOL: "No, why should it?"

MIKE: "Well, you could end up a sort of cartoon version of a punk rock band, forever trying to live up to a media image of yourselves." (A four letter word from Johnny Rotten).

MACLAREN: "No, it'll all be down to the music in the end, and the band are very serious about this aspect of it. The Sex Pistols as a punk band were bound to get this sort of treatment sooner or later—as they are the most extreme—or committed, depending on your point of view."

MIKE: "But already the tour has been a financial disaster. Ten years from now they'd have probably been given their own T.V. series, but at the moment there are things you just can't do. You can't take on the world like this and expect to come out a winner."

SEX PISTOL: "We're the spearhead of the punk movement and we're not going to compromise. We haven't lost any of the fans we had before all this fuss."

MIKE: "So it's all down to the music I haven't seen the band live, so it's difficult for me to judge. If as you say, you're going to be around a long time as a musical force, what sort of things do you play?"

MACLAREN: "As of this moment the single 'Anarchy in the U.K.' is at 41 in the charts and is going to break into the Top 30 by next week. Top of the Pops are going to have to contend with that! The band write their own stuff—it's mainly concerned with the problems of modern teenagers. Things like being bored, not having a job, trying to change society, wanting to be free, etc. It's all valid. Rock is stale at the moment. The kids want excitement not some old cabaret act like the Who or the Stones."

SEX PISTOL: "Songs like 'Problems,' 'No Future' and 'Lazy Sod' — it's all basically rock and roll."

MIKE: "Well some of those comments I'd agree with. But why be so divisive about it. We all get bored at times. Aren't we all in this together? Why make such a fascist distinction between the teenagers and anyone over that age? And why the obsession with violence?"

MACLAREN: "Violence is necessary sometimes. The aim of the music is to make the kids become angry with their lot and to give vent to their frustration. This can of course often mean a bit of violence."

And with that, the band and manager vanished to find a restaurant that would accommodate them. The Sex Pistols — perhaps the most extreme of the punk rock bands and in a way the most negative. Or just four slightly bewildered kids riding out the euphoria of attention because they don't know any different.

Having played the single 'Anarchy in the U.K.' all weekend, I still can't make up my mind as to their musical worth. Clearly they can play their instruments but whether you like how they do it is another matter.

Johnny Rotten's vocal is the big stumbling block—he sounds like a cross between Robert Wyatt and a manic Artful Dodger—and of course there's the anarchic words. I'll leave you with the reaction of my next door neighbour who I brought in as a second opinion. "Probably the end of civilisation as we know it. At least, Nero fiddled in tune!"

Legal ✓ **Decent** ✓

Don't look over your shoulder, but the Sex Pistols are coming

Sex Pistols
MARQUEE

"HURRY UP, they're having an orgy on stage," said the bloke on the door as he tore the tickets up.

I waded to the front and staightway sighted a chair arcing gracefully through the air, skidding across the stage and thudding contentedly into the PA system, to the obvious nonchalance of the bass drums and guitar.

Well I didn't think they sounded *that* bad on first earful — then I saw it was the singer wh'd done the throwing.

He was stalking round the front rows, apparently scuffing over the litter on the floor between baring his teeth at the audience and stopping to chat to members of the group's retinue. He's called Johnny Rotten and the moniker fits.

Sex Pistols? Seems I'd missed the cavortings with the two scantily clad (plastic thigh boots and bodices) pieces dancing up front. In fact, I only caught the last few numbers; enough, as it happens, to get the idea. Which is . . . a quarter of spiky teenage misfits from the wrong end of various London roads, playing 60's styled white punk rock as unself-consciously as it's possible to play it these days i.e. self-consciously.

Punks? Springsteen Bruce and the rest of 'em would get shredded if they went up against these boys. They've played less than a dozen gigs as yet, have a small but fanatic following, and don't get asked back. Next month they play the Institute of Contemporary Arts if that's a clue.

I'm told the Pistols repertoire includes lesser known Dave Berry and Small Faces numbers (check out early Kinks' B sides leads), besides an Iggy and the Stooges item and several self-penned numbers like the moronic "I'm Pretty Vacant," a meandering power-chord job that produced the chair-throwing incident.

No-one asked for an encore but they did one anyway: "We're going to play 'Substitute'."

"You can't play," heckled an irate French punter.

"So what?" countered the bassman, jutting his chin in the direction of the bewildered Frog.

That's how it is with the Pistols — a musical experience with the emphasis on Experience.

"Actually, we're not into music," one of the Pistols confided afterwards.

Wot then?

"We're into chaos."

Neil Spencer

Pistols' Johnny Rotten: it fits.

SEX PISTOLS, MR GEORGE'S, COVENTRY, 17TH DECEMBER 1977

**TOM ROBINSON BAND,
BARBARELLA'S, BIRMINGHAM,
3RD NOVEMBER 1977**

ADVERTS, BIRMINGHAM,
19TH NOVEMBER 1977

Pop world has its eye on Gaye

A JOURNALIST'S daughter is heading for the big-time — but whether she or her group want themselves feted is anybody's guess.

The lady is Gaye Advert, bass player with first-time chart occupants, The Adverts. The Adverts belong with the new wave rock scene and their single, Looking Through Gary Gilmore's Eyes, is fast becoming the single few radio stations will programme.

Gaye has just had her 21st birthday, an event which was mainly punctuated by her seeing The Adverts appear on Top Of The Pops.

She is strong in looks and with her black hair, black nail polish and black eye make-up plus the mandatory new wave gear is in danger of making people concentrate on her than any bass playing ability she may possess, let alone the sound of The Adverts.

She denies their hit is sick. "We were fascinated by the story around Gary Gilmore and the fact that he gave his eyes. We made this song and I suppose the tune is catchy."

She says there is sometimes a narrow line between controversial and worthwhile discs and those which are plain nasty. She does not think Looking Through Gary Gilmore's Eyes belongs in the latter category.

Gaye is bashful about explaining her bass playing. "I'm a learner, I want to get better," and she says she would like to be seen as a person who belongs with a group.

GAYE ADVERT—"I want to be treated like one of the group."

The reluctant glamour girls of punk rock

By James Johnson

PUNK rock has frequently been described as anti-glamour and anti-romance. But the new revolution in rock music has nevertheless produced two ladies who could be described as the first sex symbols of punk.

Both Debbie Harry of New York group Blondie and Gaye Advert of the Adverts have often been used as pin-up material in punk magazines and have become accustomed to receiving a large number of letters each week from male punk admirers.

However, this new role that has been thrust upon the girls makes them a little reluctant and uncertain.

"I never think of myself as a woman," says bass player Gaye. "It's got nothing to do with music. I just want to be known as one of the group and treated like them."

Singer Debbie Harry agrees: "I've always wanted to be part of a group like this but all the boys in New York would discourage me.

"They said a girl could only make it in cabaret or as a sex symbol. I don't want that. Why shouldn't I be able to work on a lot of other levels, just like a guy?"

DEBBIE HARRY

THE DAMNED, TOP RANK SUITE, BIRMINGHAM, 21ST NOVEMBER 1977

SUCHENTS PRESENTS
THE DAMNED
(featuring Rat Scabies and Captain Sensible)
IN HULL COLLEGE OF EDUCATION
COTTINGHAM ROAD AUDITORIUM
Friday, March 30th, 8.30 p.m.–12.30 a.m.
Late Bar
£1.25 in advance, £1.50 at the door
Available from Bofs, Shakespeare Records and all Student Union Shops

DAMNED AND BLASTED

The Damned — Red Cow, Hammersmith

A working class hero is something to be. John Lennon said that a long time back — and it's only now that the long-waited musical revolution is taking place.

Peace, love and flowers are well and truly dead. Enter aggression, rebellion and angry energy with the new-wave bands responsible for the current phenomenon known as punk-rock.

One of the foremost groups in the movement is The Damned, an outfit formed about four months ago who judge the success of each gig by the amount of chaos caused.

By their own standards, last week's gig at the Hammersmith Red Cow was disappointing. By anyone else's standards, it was a devastating assault on eyes and ears that was charged with an excitement and urgency missing for far too long from the complacent world of jetset rock.

Musical expertise is irrelevant. What does count is the violent, passionate energy that shakes bones and stands hair on end.

There were few smiling faces at the Red Cow. Everyone was stalking around looking mean and menacing, dressed in the peculiar fashions born from the arrival of the new music. Like their heroes.

Dave Vanium, vocalist, was wearing leathers, dark glasses and a permanent sneer. Bassist Captain Sensible walked on with a gag in his mouth and a pair of shades with vividly-coloured, plastic-like frames. Brian James pointed his guitar menacingly and Rat Scabies was banging the blazes out of his drums.

It was atmospheric, all right. The Damned and groups like them have given an ailing music scene a violent shot of real, life-saving anarchy.

Captain Sensible after the show: "There are guys down there who want to beat our heads in. Violence makes me want to hit someone. They should call me Captain Chaos..."

what was said during

The Damned ... on the edge.

© Alan Perry

ROCK: James Johnson

THE BOISTEROUS pushing and relentless pogo dancing that is all part of a good night out for punk rock fans, has now obviously become a lucrative, marketable commodity in itself.

"Come back tomorrow night for another evening of chaos," urged the disc jockey at the Sundown last night after the **Damned** had been hauled off stage in the interests of safety. "Membership is only £1," he added.

Indeed, strict codes of behaviour that give punk rock its attraction as an instant social scene for young people, almost puts music in second place as simply the catalyst that holds it all together.

The Damned are one of the earliest pioneers of the new wave and continue to attract a heavy duty punk audience without ever having had to churn out the bold, somewhat naive political rhetoric favoured by some of their competitors.

The group consists of vocalist Dave Vanian, guitarist Brian James, drummer Rat Scabies, bass player Captain Sensible and a new guitarist apparently only known as Lu.

Together they performed with the impression they are living on the absolute edge of some outer limit—an essential ingredient for a punk rock group.

Facing a ferocious audience spitting out their appreciation, Vanian threw h i m s e l f heroically into their midst. The pale oval face, jet-black hair and deep-set made-up eyes resembles a form of embryo Dracula.

Playing with 100 per cent guts and brio, the group emphasised their position as one of the leaders of the most natural and spontaneous movement that has occurred in rock music for 10 years.

uage."

ERLEND CLOUSTON on the pop cult that caused a storm

- THE DAMNED: With Captain Sensible and Rat Scabies.
- JOHNNY ROTTEN: The barmaids like him anyway.

They're pop's storm-troopers

THE 'SUNDAY TIMES', foaming at the mouth, called them "anti-life." Yesterday's Daily Mirror came up with "dirty, obnoxious, and arrogant." The object of all this righteous attention? Not the Provisional IRA nor the next KGB delegation, but that curious hiccup of the musical world—Punk Rock.

Well, I'm sorry to disappoint you. The most sinister thing about Punk Rock is the ease with which the media has been manipulated into projecting precisely the sort of image Punk Rockers have sought.

At the same time, the media, by remaining transfixed by the creature of its own imagination has by and large completely missed the significance of the movement's genuine impact on the music business.

MYTH NO. 1: Punk Rock is about VIOLENCE.

It is but no more and no less than any other popular music craze has been. There have been fights at Punk Rock concerts, but fists have been raised at folk get togethers before now.

Local promoters Roger Eagle and Ken Testi, who are just completing a sort of Punk Rock season at Eric's, their Matthew Street club, have lost only a couple of beer mugs in two months. "Sure, there's plenty of activity on stage," says Testi, "but nothing outrageous."

Of course, this does not prevent journalists passing on anecdotes that they may be fed. Cannibalism is about the only crime that hasn't been placed at the door of Johnny Rotten, lead singer of the Sex Pistols. Yet Eagle and Testi found him amenable, if short on conversation. "Our barmaid thought him most sweet."

THE SEX PISTOLS shoot their mouths off on television and switchboards are jammed with protests ... one man kicked in his £380 colour set ... the whole incident has dragged Punk Rock all over the headlines. We put Britain's newest pop phenomenon into perspective.

Yesterday's headlines—"fury" and "filth".

Similarly, Rat Scabies, drummer with the dreaded Damned, was "an exceptionally nice guy." We talked to him for hours."

MYTH NO. 2 Punk Rock contributes nothing to contemporary music.

At a superficial level, this appears to hold some truth. The stock Punk sound is hard and fast and fairly repetitive, offering nothing that the Who or the Rolling Stones weren't selling ten years ago.

Yet there is exactly the point. The Who and the Rolling Stones have become revered gurus of the pop cult, staging extravagant concerts according to the Anglo-Saxon deity calendar, lingering most often in the places and with the people completely foreign to the lower-working class wallets that linked the two.

Punk takes a positive pride in being accessible to the masses—hence the display of Salvation Army clothing whenever a Punk band takes the stage. They take a cheeky delight in being "average" musicians—and in using below average language to journalists.

Superceding all this in importance though is the profound effect Punk's emergence has had on the people who by and large control British popular music: the big record company-promoter-management tie-up."

According to the unwritten rules, bands without vast financial backing shall not make a name for themselves. Punk said sucks to that and ground off round the country in battered buggies, playing wherever they could find a promoter fast-moving enough to book them in.

Unlike other groups, they demanded no 'advance.'

No-one wanted to know The Damned, so they raised £350 to make a record privately then touted it round individual record shops. 'New Rose' sold 4,000 copies inside a week and is now at No. 65 in the national charts. In almost indecent haste, EMI moguls laid down £40,000 to sign up our silent Johnny Rotten's Sex Pistols, top co-Punkers with The Damned.

Until then, it was safe to say that 'Punk' equalled 'Poverty.' "We had The Stranglers up from London once," recalls Eagle, "and they had to go back that night at 40 m.p.h. in a converted ice cream van. They didn't have enough money to stay in a hotel."

Kicking the door open

It won't, of course, last much longer. The kids will desert the bands once the Establishment moves in and makes them respectable, like they did with Presley, Rhythm and Blues, and the psychedelic groups. Already Punk's 'sharecropper' look is finding its way on to the fashion pages.

"They are the shock troops, though," Eagle says. "They've kicked the doors open and frightened a few people. I think music—popular music—is going to be very much in their debt a few years from now."

It's a Damned good single

THE DAMNED: "New / Help" (Stiff Records).
CLOVER: "Chicken Funk" (Vertigo).
HANK MIZELL: "Rakin and Scrapin' Higher" (Charly).

Best single I've heard for some time is from the Damned crucify in 102 the new phenomenon "punk rock", which I was explaining last week.

Subtle the Damned are not, "New Rose" is a one-chord song enlivened by blistering guitar, pounding drums and manic vocals. It nearly blew my headphones off, and might cause brain damage among the unwary.

On the other side, the damned crucify in 102 seconds any notions of good taste John Lennon and Paul McCartney might have had about their song "Help."

It's taken at a breakneck garbled pace, I imagine it's a pointed comment on the generation gap, and at least it's over quickly if not painlessly.

© Alan Perry

MIKE LLOYD MUSIC Rock Concerts

VICTORIA HALL HANLEY

MONDAY, DECEMBER 12th
PLEASE NOTE NEW DATE
7.30 p.m.

BOOMTOWN RATS
BOOMTOWN RATS
BOOMTOWN RATS

with Guest Group

£1.60 in advance (£2.00 on the door)

THURSDAY, DECEMBER 15th
7.30 p.m.

THE JAM
THE JAM
THE JAM

£1.60 in advance (£2.00 on the door)

Tickets available from MIKE LLOYD RECORD SHOPS, Hanley, Tunstall, Newcastle. 268...

Eric's Mathew St. 236-7881
MEMBERS' NOTICE

TONIGHT 8.30 p.m.–2 a.m.
BUZZCOCKS
plus The Fall, and Eddie Bep
Members 90p   Guests £1.20

SAT 19th 8.30 p.m.–2 a.m.
THE REZILLOS
plus The Pleasers
Members 75p   Guests £1

SUN 8 p.m.–11.30 p.m.
FIVE HAND REEL
Members 75p   Guests £1

MON 21st 7.30–12.30 p.m.
Reggae Music
BLACK SLATE
with special guests
BIG IN JAPAN
Members 90p   Guests £1.20
plus Jah Quaminah Hi-Fi

WED 7.30–12.30 p.m.
ELECTRIC CHAIRS
plus Alternative T.V.
Members 90p   Guests £1.20

Tickets for Southside, Johnny, Ian Drury, and Ultravox now on sale, Midday–2 p.m.

POST, MONDAY, MAY 30 1977

COLSTON HALL
TONIGHT at 7.30

Double 'M' Promotions presents

FROM NEW YORK

RAMONES

In the Charts this week at No. 22
'SHEENA IS A PUNK ROCKER'

Plus

TALKING HEADS

£1.80   £1.50   £1.20   90p

Back to

8—EVENING STANDARD, TUESDAY, JUNE 14, 1977

As punk hits number one, two 'new' bands have new ideas

Fans shoot outrageous Pistols into the top spot

By Paul Taylor

THE ESTABLISHMENT hates them. They can't set foot on stage and their records are banned, but the Sex Pistols are punk rock's number one and their fans have proved it.

Banned from TV networks, radio stations and some shops, the Sex Pistols' outrageous record God Save the Queen has sold more than 200,000 copies and locks set to earn the group a silver disc later this week.

This week the record that accuses the Queen of being "a moron" tops the New Musical Express poll and is high in the British Market Research Bureau and Capital Radio charts.

This week the record tops the New Musical Express chart, is number four in a chart used by the BBC, and number nine in Melody Maker.

The universal banning of the disc has probably helped sales to an unrivalled peak. The only other record to make No 1 after being banned was Je t'aim—with heavy breathing from Jane Birkin and Serge Gainsborough which topped the charts more than seven years ago.

Malcolm McLaren, who manages the Sex Pistols said: "I think it is great. It goes to show that whatever the industry has thought of the disc, and even if they think of the Pistols as a bunch of trouble-makers who can't play some 200,000 kids disagree.

"Whether one agrees with the sentiments of the disc, kids have bought it."

He said he thought the disc would have become "the fastest-selling record in history" had it not been banned.

But the record's success will not make the Pistols rich. Mr McLaren estimates that the profit margin on each 70p disc is only 6p.

"Most of the money is owed to Virgin. I doubt very much whether the Pistols will make £20,000 out of it."

Controversy

The disc could have sparked off another controversy, for Virgin Records are concerned about the two-place drop to No. 4 shown in today's British Market Research Bureau's charts.

Al Clark, of Virgin Records, who signed the group on a £45,000 contract and produced the record, said: "Every sales survey suggests that the Pistols record is the best-selling single in the country.

"It could make a silver disc by the end of the week."

Virgin Records executives were meeting the bureau today to discuss the situation.

The Sex Pistols are the first new wave punk rock groups to appear early last year.

They first achieved notoriety after a Thames Television which offended many viewers.

Malcolm McLaren says the group are still banned from British stages, "but we plan something on water soon," he said.

● Punk rock concerts have been banned from St Albans following a performance of The Clash, when a crowd of 500 had to be turned away outside the town hall after all tickets had been sold.

● The Knebworth Pop Festival has been postponed until August because of difficulties over who will appear. The original date was July 2.

How they compile the charts

By Liz Gill

THE Top 20 position of the Sex Pistols' hit God Save the Queen highlights a problem faced all the time in the music business—just how accurate are the charts?

It all depends, say the chart compilers, on the method you use.

Both major music papers, the New Musical Express and Melody Maker, get their information from record shops and then work out positions on a points scale.

"This means our shops send us their Top 20 based on over-the-counter sales and then we give the top record 20 points, the second 19 and so on," said a spokesman for the NME. The points — not the total sales—are then added up to give the Top 20.

"So the success of a record doesn't necessarily bear a true relation to the number sold. You could sell only 20 in one shop and still be top there.

"But it would be impossible to total up every record sold in every shop in the country.

"We just try and get a representative selection, like an opinion poll."

Roy Burchell, charts editor of Melody Maker, agrees. He puts his charts together from information from 200 shops all over the country.

"You get differences between charts because of the shops. For instance, shops in some areas might be very keen on soul. And when you get a record like the Sex Pistols, then some shops aren't carrying it at all so that obviously affects its points, he said.

he British Market Research Bureau, which supplies the BBC, Music Week and several record companies, bases its charts on the total number of sales for each record.

Senior executive Ros Garner said: "We have a panel of 300 record outlets right across the country, chosen to be representative of area and size. They send us a list of every record they sell.

"Then all the adding up is done by computer and the number one is the one with the most records actually sold.

GREAT SILVER JUBILEE LP RECORD SALE

TOP 60 SPECIALS

	Normal	Our Price	Save
Abba—Arrival	3·79	2·50	1·29
Jack Jones—All To Yourself	3·49	1·99	1·50*
Peter Gabriel—Peter Gabriel	3·50	2·25	1·25
Best of the Faces—The Faces	4·99	3·49	1·50*
Pink Floyd—Animals	3·60	2·50	1·10
Supertramp—Even in the Quietest Moments	3·60	1·99	1·61
Beatles—Live at the Hollywood Bowl	3·35	1·99	1·36*
Don Williams—Visions	3·39	2·50	89p
Status Quo—Live	4·99	3·49	1·50
Barry W... Hits Vol. 2	3·50	1·99	1·51*
	3·25	2·50.	75p

...S SAVINGS ON:
...tel California, Rock Follies 77, 10 cc—Deceptive ...s Born, Little Feat—Time Loves a Hero, etc. etc.

...ettes must be cleared from 25p!

...DS & TAPES
...sement,
...derwoods, Tottenham Ct. Road end)
... late night Thursday

...AT

...S & TAPES
...C.2. Open Monday-Friday.
...tticoat Lane) Open Mon.-Fri. and SUNDAY
... to availability

STEWART (left) and Gouldman of 10cc . . . like starting all over again.

10cc rock back from the grave

By Charles Catchpole

"FIVE CC indeed—20 cc more like!" The speaker is Graham Gouldman, songwriter, bass player and founder member of 10 cc. The target for his scorn: the cynics who a few months ago had declared the most ambitious and inventive of British bands dead and buried.

The derisory nickname "5cc" was bestowed on Gouldman and guitarist-vocalist Eric Stewart after the traumatic departure of the other half of the band, Lol Creme and Kevin Godley, to develop a new-fangled, electronical-musical hybrid known as the gizmo.

The band, whose intelligent, "up-market" approach to pop produced such masterpieces as I'm Not In Love and I'm Mandy, Fly Me, drawing comparisons with the Beach Boys and The Beatles, had apparently suffered a fatal blow.

Sterner stuff

But Stewart and Gouldman, 10 years in the pop business apiece, didn't agree. They went straight into their own recording studio, Strawberry South in downtown Dorking, and came up with two hit singles, Things We Do For Love and Good Morning Judge, and a widely-praised LP, Deceptive Bends. They then recruited three new members, rehearsed for a grand total of three and a half weeks, and—with some trepidation—hit the road.

The applause of an ecstatic audience was still ringing down the corridors of Sheffield City Hall as Gouldman dropped into a chair and spoke about the band's comeback tour, which reaches its climax with three consecutive gigs starting on Saturday at the Hammersmith Odeon.

"The reviews say it, the audiences say it, and we all feel it. This band is streets ahead of the old one. It's like starting all over again. There's an air of excitement which I haven't felt in years," he said.

Stewart added: "We never dreamed the new band would gell so quickly. We had just a few weeks, not only to reach a stage which had taken the last band four years to achieve, but if possible to surpass it. And I think we've done it."

Stewart (formerly of the Mindbenders and Hotlegs), and Gouldman (writer of hits for Herman's Hermits, the Yardbirds, the Hollies etc), have retained 10cc's tour drummer Paul Burgess, and added ex-arrival and Kokomo pianist Tony O'Malley, Pilot drummer Stuart Tosh, and a young guitarist from Cambridge, Rick Fenn.

The new men have added an extra dimension to the old band's adventurous, subtle but sometimes introverted songs.

"We were a sterile band" admitted Stewart. "We were always trying to be perfectionists. It may sound a strange thing to say, but we were too musically-orientated."

"We used to be highly critical of everything we did, almost paranoid, in fact" said Gouldman. "Now we're more stage-orientated, we're looser. We can relax more. We don't care about the odd mistake. In fact someone made one this evening which, in the old days, we would have argued about for hours. Now it's just part of the excitement of developing afresh."

A Union Jack among the swastikas

WHO are these weirdos, slouching into the lounge bar of the pub in respectable, semi-detached, suburban Whitton?

There are gaunt-faced boys with spiky, lavatory-brush hair, tight leather trousers and pink vests; girls with safety pin ear-rings, two-tone razor cuts and eyes made up like Cat Woman (writes Charles Catchpole).

IT'S THE PUNKS! Time to gulp down your half of sparkling CO2 and head for the safety of Acacia Avenue.

But wait. Aren't those Union Jacks among the swastikas? And badges of the Queen? Carnaby Street has infiltrated the New Wave. The Jam are in town.

The Jam are odd, even among the oddities of the punk rock scene. For a start they shun the word punk, although punks follow them in swarms. They're all 19, and play the loud, furious music that has become known as New Wave. Yet many of their songs are lifted from the despised Sixties.

Oddest thing of all, they don't display any of the fashionable anti-monarchy, anti-society, anti-everything that moves attitudes of most New Wave bands.

PAUL WELLER — rock is fun.

They're actually playing free at two Jubilee concerts in Tower Hamlets on Saturday and Battersea the following week.

This smacks of a carefully contrived anti-punk stance.

"Not at all," says guitarist Paul Weller. "We're not worried about what's in or out. We just thought it would be a nice idea to do the gigs.

Paul Weller is obviously going to be a star.

He wrote most of the songs on the group's debut LP (just out) including the hit single In The City, hailed by the cognoscenti as the best New Wave record yet.

His musical philosophy is simple. "Rock is supposed to be fun, something to dance to, to unwind you at the end of the day. All this sociological crap that has been talked about punk, all this deep significance it has been given, makes me laugh. We don't pretend we won't change. If things go well for us we're bound to. But we'll always try to stay close to our fans. That's really what punk, New Wave, call it what you will, is all about. Accessibility."

ALBUM REVIEW

MEAL TICKET, as readers of this paper must know by now, are the best live band in London. Ironically, this does not help their debut LP, Code of the Road (EMI).

It's a lovely album, crammed with inventive, melodic songs, at least six of which ought to be Top Ten singles. But it doesn't quite capture the unique live qualities of the band.

For those unfortunates who haven't seen them, though, it's a gem. The songs, by keyboard player Ric Jones and lyricist Dave Pierce, tell of various aspects of life on the road, from being broke and busted (Keeping the Faith) to being messed around by agents and promoters (Day Job).

The words are witty, the tunes maddeningly catchy, the harmonies faultless. The whole thing is beautifully paced. It's one of the best first albums I've heard. How about a live one next?

tive presence of far too many nervous and over-zealous security guards. — Beatrice

EVENING STANDARD, TUESDAY, MAY 10, 1977—3

I wanna riot! Fans smash 200 seats at punk show

NEWS ON CAMERA

REPORT: James Johnson
PICTURES: Chris Moorhouse

THE LATEST revolution in rock music exploded into disorder once again when the largest punk rock 'new wave' concert yet seen in London was staged at the Rainbow Theatre last night.

As top-of-the-bill group The Clash closed the four hour show, more than 200 seats were demolished by the audience in a bout of rowdy fanaticism.

The house lights were turned up but The Clash contined to play on regardless.

White Riot—I Wanna Riot thundered vocalist Joe Strummer, shuddering violently, as the broken seats tumbled up on to the stage beside him.

A search of the arriving audience had revealed a battery of items like knives, iron bars and assorted chains.

Release

The people who looked out of place were the gaggles of record company executives seated at the rear of the theatre, but their presence underlined the fact that punk rock has now become big business.

Despite the scorn and ridicule that accompanied the emergence of the new style, it has now become evident that punk, or new wave rock, has become the fastest growing commodity in the music business.

The Clash's first album entered the Top Twenty last month in its first week of release and was quickly followed into the charts by a record from another new wave group, The Stranglers.

"It's unprecedented for new albums by any group to get into the charts so quickly," said Maurice Oberstien, the British managing director of CBS Records.

"The record business has been looking around for a long time for something new, and this has to be it.

"I know people can be horrified by punk rock, but personally I am sanguine about the whole situation. For every person who says 'I hate it', you are going to find somebody who reacts the opposite way.

"I remember the days when the public was horrified by the Bill Haley-Elvis Presley era. Punk rock is just a new fashion and a new music. It is perfectly harmless."

To the ever-growing numbers of new wave fans, The Clash, from West London, have become known as the ultimate expression of an angry form of quasi-political nihilism.

The songs are blank negative diatribes against "high-rise blocks, unemployment and general urban decay."

Guitarist Mick Jones once claimed that he had never lived below the 17th floor.

Their music has been dubbed the Sound of the Westway. A spluttering, high-speed, manic rush, it displays a release of energy normally stifled by living in Britain during an economic depression.

Groups like The Clash have suddenly emerged on the basis that there is probably more for young people to protest about in 1977 than in the 1960s.

None of the current new wave groups could claim to be great musicians or lyricists but last night's show and recent record sales suggest that they have become more relevant to a proportion of young rock audiences than superstar vocalists or virtuoso musicians.

● **Original 'New Wave' band moves quietly along — centre pages.**

RIP IT UP... Punk fans tear up seats and hurl them towards the stage.

PUNK PROTEST..."quasi-political nihilism."

THE CLASH play on as broken seats land on the stage.

Thoughts of the punk philosopher

JEAN - JACQUES Burnel cultivates the public image of a man who has graduated from pulling the wings off flies to beating up old ladies, writes **Charles Catchpole**.

On stage he clutches his bass guitar like a flame thrower, mean and macho, glowering and leering, in a battered leather jacket and dirty jeans.

He is one of the reasons why the Stranglers, most successful of the punk/new wave groups, are banned from town halls, thrown out of hotels and harassed in the streets.

Off-stage, he is quietly spoken, almost introverted, articulate and knowledgeable on a range of subjects, including philosophy and economics.

He studied economics in college and planned to teach karate—until he met Hugh Cornwell and decided to found the Stranglers a little over two years ago.

Paranoia

Nervous promoters have cancelled 11 dates so far on the group's first nation-wide tour, and Burnel, 23-year-old son of French immigrants, reels them off with something like pride.

"It's punk-bashing season," he says. "Paranoia is on the march. Do you know, we were eating in a restaurant in Plymouth the other day—just eating, not fighting or spitting—and the police came in and supervised our meal.

"They stood and watched over us until we had finished. Can you imagine it? Don't you think they'd have something better to do?"

But surely the Stranglers, with their bizarre appearance and threatening stance, go out of their way to provoke such reactions?

Burnel grins. "Well, you have to be a bit outrageous to get noticed. But honestly, we've cooled down a lot in the last two years.

"We used to have whole audiences walking out on us..."

The Stranglers, who play two concerts at the Round House, Chalk Farm, on Sunday, have little difficulty getting noticed. At a recent London gig the GLC pulled the plug out on them, offended by what it considered to be a naughty word on singer Hugh Cornwell's T-shirt.

The row which followed provided invaluable headlines, as did Burnel's starring role in a Sunday newspaper "exposure" of the punk horror.

"They said my hands were a mass of bleeding cuts and weeping sores. Well, they're not, are they," he said, dramatically spreading them to draw attention to a neat manicure.

The article, which would have had most punks foaming at the mouth, did not greatly upset Burnel, however.

"It was an ignorant appraisal, but I don't suppose it did much harm," he said. "It helps people to identify their positions on an issue. It probably also helps the sale of our album..."

The ambivalent attitude of the Stranglers to such issues is demonstrated by their appearance on Top of the Pops, the scorned shrine of safe, establishment rock.

The Stranglers' blend of fashionable punk attitude with sound commercial sense has paid off.

Theeir single Peaches, a joyous ode to male chauvinism, which has infuriated women's libbers, is the biggest selling new wave single after the Pistols' anti-monarchy diatribe, and their debut album is as high in the LP charts.

If they do something naughty and the GLC switches them off on Sunday it will probably go to number one

JEAN-JACQUES BURNEL—on stage, mean and macho; off stage, quiet and introvert.

THE STRANGLERS, THE LOCARNO BALLROOM, 4TH OCTOBER, 1977.

© Alan Perry

© Alan Perry

WAYNE COUNTY, DE MONTFORT HALL, LEICESTER, NOVEMBER 1977

Punk rockers' £100 clash with the law

A CLASH with the law cost two leading punk rock musicians £100 after they admitted stealing from an exclusive North-East hotel.

But yesterday lead singer John Mellor, alias Joe Strummer and Nick Headon the drummer in the punk rock band, The Clash, said their experiences in police cells would lead to a new song.

Their brush with the law started when eight pillows, a towel and a hotel key disappeared from the Commonwealth Holiday Inn at Seaton Burn on May 21. The band were staying there after their concert at Newcastle University.

Police investigations took detectives down to Hertfordshire where the group were interviewed.

Two group members were put on police bail but failed to appear at Morpeth on June 3 because they could not afford to miss part of their nationwide concert tour.

But when Strummer was arrested for criminal damage in London, Headon gave himself up and they returned to Morpeth under police escort.

Morpeth magistrates fined Strummer (24), of Forest Hill, London, £60 for taking the pillows and the towel worth £26.

Headon (22) who admitted theft of a hotel key and key ring, was fined £40.

Strummer told police the pillows were taken to make the group's return to London more comfortable. Headon asked for four other offences involving hotel keys to be considered.

The Stranglers head West

THE Stranglers — easily the best thing to come out of the New Wave so far — play two gigs in Devon as part of their massive tour which starts soon.

The band — banned by Torbay council in June — are playing at the Fiesta in Plymouth on Sunday, October 9, and at Exeter University the next night.

Tickets for the Plymouth concert are already on sale, but it will be a couple of weeks before they are available in Exeter.

Sex Pistol goes into hiding

By James Johnson

SEX PISTOL Sid Vicious was in hiding today after an incident with the police at a London hotel on Tuesday night.

Police were called to the Ambassadors Hotel when guests heard smashing in a room occupied by Vicious and his new wife Nancy.

Substances were later taken from the room by police for analysis and staff at the hotel were reported to have said that the room was covered with glass and blood.

"We don't know where he is," said a spokesman for the Sex Pistols record company, Virgin, today.

"I'm sure he will be keeping out of the way to avoid the repercussions that come after this kind of thing.

"Our dealings with the group are only limited to their careers. What Sid does in his private life is his own affair."

The Sex Pistols office in London also refused to disclose where Sid Vicious was staying.

Sex Pistol man sacked

BASS player Glenn Matlock of the Sex Pistols, has been given the sack and replaced by another punk rocker Sid Vicious.

According to manager Malcolm MacLaren: "Glenn Matlock was thrown out of the Sex Pistols so I'm told because he went on too long about Paul McCartney. EMI was enough. The Beatles were too much."

ROCK

BUZZCOCKS, Siouxsie, the Banshees and Subway Sect are playing in a raunchy punk concert at the Roundhouse, Chalk Farm Road, on Sunday at 5.30 p.m., £1·80. Wayne County and Electric Chairs plus Menace plus Skunks and Backlash appear at the Vortex in Wardour Street on Monday. Adam and the Ants are at the Marquee on Sunday and the Fabulous Poodles plus Lesser Known Tunisians are at Chelsea College, Manresa Road, S.W.3 tomorrow (£1·25).

EVENING STANDARD news focus on the first twelve months of punk

Who's made it in the year of the safety-pin

By Charles Catchpole

EXACTLY a year ago this week, the Evening Standard drew up the curtain on "a style of music loosely known as punk rock.

Was it, we wondered, "a new cultural phenomenon or just a giant confidence trick?"

Twelve months on, the question is still unanswered. But one thing is certain—punk rock, now dignified with the title "new wave," has given a complacent music business its biggest fright since the start of rock 'n' roll. And they said THAT wouldn't last either...

THE SEX PISTOLS started it all, though their roots can be traced back several years to prototype punks from America like Lou Reed, Iggy Pop and the New York Dolls. They CAN play—though like the Stones before them, they rapidly realised that playing dumb can get more attention than playing well. Judgment must be reserved until the release of their first LP (due next month).

THE STRANGLERS are far and away the most proficient and the most successful of the new wave bands, with a string of single success and two chart topping LPs. An organ sound borrowed from The Doors and a bass guitar elevated to the level of a lead instrument makes them immediately identifiable among the morass of mediocre punk sound-alikes. Their big test will come with their third album.

GAYE ADVERT—catchiest record.

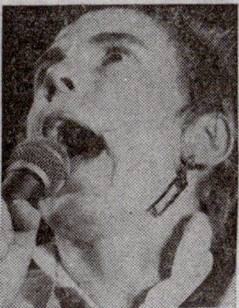

JOHNNY ROTTEN—started it all.

THE CLASH are the purist punks' idols. They supported the Pistols at London's first —and last—punk festival at the 100 Club just over a year ago, and won acclaim for their highly "political" songs like White Riot. Their latest single Complete Control, is one of the best punk numbers; ironically it's about their own struggles with their record company to win control of their material — a measure of how far the "straight" music business has gone to assimilate punk culture.

THE DAMNED are the last of the "big four" of punk—and the first to hit an identity crisis. Their mannered stage appearance — in particular vocalist Dave Vanian's vampire image—has worn thin at a time when straightforwardness and simplicity are the order of the day. Drummer Rat Scabies has walked out in a huff, and their recent refusal to play at a punk festival when the fee was not forthcoming in advance has reinforced suspicions that the new wave is just young people with old values.

DR. FEELGOOD may be a bit old to be classed as new wave, but they were among the first bands to revive the seedy, sweaty feel of r'n'b which lent much impetus to the punk explosion. They have no pretensions towards anything except havin' a good time. Product of Canvey Island, along with such other straightforward rip-roaring funsters as The Rods and Lew Lewis, they are rooted firmly in the boozy, billigerent, no-frills tradition of the Animals

GENERATION X: Probably the best of the up-and-coming new wavers. Visually strong, with vocalist Billy Idol drawing comparisons with such as Heinz and Billy Fury, they shun on-stage posing, and are not ashamed to do "old" numbers (like John Lennon's Gimme Some Truth.

THE JAM are unique in a scene which thrives on its brand of conformity. Clean-cut, conservative Small Faces? Who look alike, they blend 60s excitement (and sometimes songs) with 70s energy and "take us or leave us" approach. Guitarist Paul Weller is one of the strongest musicians/writers/personalities to emerge since his hero Pete Townsend. Pistols borrowed his electric riff from In The City for their new single Holidays In The Sun.

THE ADVERTS have made the catchiest, most commercial new wave record yet, the clever Gary Gilmore's Eyes. Also in their repertoire, the tongue-in-cheek One Chord Wonders. Strong on image (bass player Gaye Advert is one of the few girls act on the punk scene), their act gains added charm from a tendency to verge on an amiable shambles.

THE TOM ROBINSON BAND could never be called punk, but their politically "up front" stance has earned them a place as pacemakers of the new wave. Leader Robinson has twigged that sloganising is an instant turn-off, so he makes his points about facism, oppression, discrimination, etc., simply and subtly in the framework of good, catchy tunes. It takes skill to do a song about homosexuality (Glad To Be Gay) without making it preaching, embarrasing or boring.

XTC are most people's tip for future. Cool, wry, humourous, their music is a million years from the wham-bam, chain-saw monotony of the run-of-the-mill punk bands. Behind the sharp haircuts and the popping eyes is a slick cleverness that has overtones of the despised art school scene

THE BOOMTOWN RATS combine the heavy, full-frontal sensuality of the early Stones with a desire to entertain in the broadest sense which is pure vaudeville. Bigger than the average punk band (six in all), musically accomplished, they are further blessed with the added ingredient of personality in the larger-than-life shape of singer Bob Geldof. The next Stranglers, some say.

THE BEST OF THE REST

Elvis Costello, Ian Dury, Nick Lowe, Wreckless Eric: the oddball package from Stiff Records, currently touring the country under the title A Bunch of Stiffs. Various ages, styles, degrees of eccentricity, add up to proof of the new wave maxim that you don't have to be beautiful to be a star.

Gloria Mundi: punk meets glam-rock, and—amazingly—they hit it off. Singer Eddie combines the staginess of Bowie with the ferocity of Rotten.

The Motors: punk meets rock 'n' roll and everyone has a party.

Band told: Push off

By Lynda Murdin

THE NEW single by the group Electric Chairs is to be supplied under the counter in plain brown paper wrappers—because major record companies have refused to have anything to do with it. They do not like its title or lyrics.

A new label has been created —The Sweet FA Label—and friends of the group are busy sticking the labels on by hand and plan to distribute 30,000 copies themselves.

"Really it's just fun, but everybody takes it so seriously," said a spokesman. The title? A well-known expletive.

HORNES
for your life style
...we've got the clothes
West End, City, Croydon, Watford

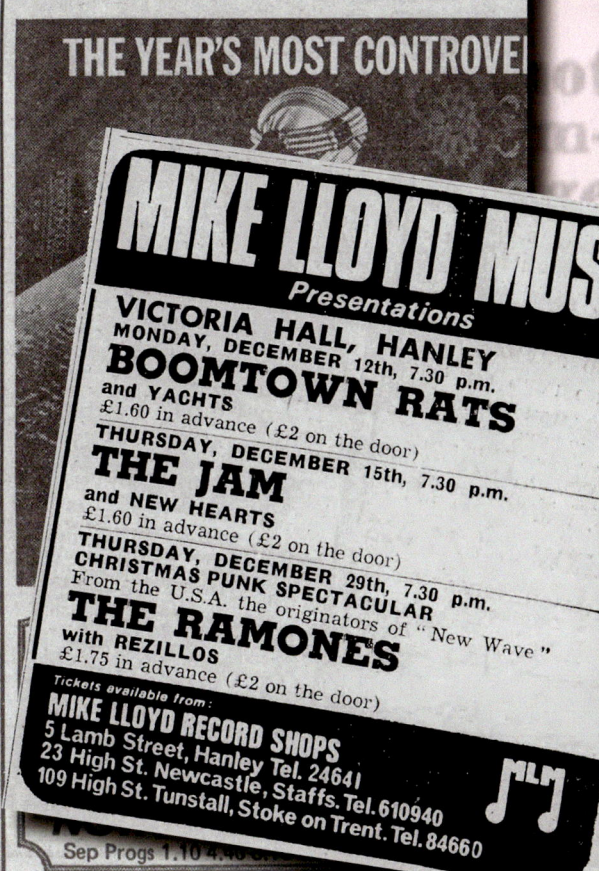

MIKE LLOYD MUSIC Presentations

VICTORIA HALL, HANLEY
MONDAY, DECEMBER 12th, 7.30 p.m.
BOOMTOWN RATS
and YACHTS
£1.60 in advance (£2 on the door)

THURSDAY, DECEMBER 15th, 7.30 p.m.
THE JAM
and NEW HEARTS
£1.60 in advance (£2 on the door)

THURSDAY, DECEMBER 29th, 7.30 p.m.
CHRISTMAS PUNK SPECTACULAR
From the U.S.A. the originators of "New Wave"
THE RAMONES
with REZILLOS
£1.75 in advance (£2 on the door)

Tickets available from:
MIKE LLOYD RECORD SHOPS
5 Lamb Street, Hanley Tel. 24641
23 High St. Newcastle, Staffs. Tel. 610940
109 High St. Tunstall, Stoke on Trent. Tel. 84660

Short and sweet

PEOPLE leaving the Jam concert at Derby King's Hall last Friday were left with two distinct feelings; elation at having witnessed possibly Britain's most exciting touring band, and disappointment at not seeing more of them.

The Jam, a three-piece outfit who dress like the early Who and at times sound remarkably like them, came on stage and played as if they were under contract to burn up as much energy as possible. Fair enough.

But when the effort expended meant the concert lasted merely 40 minutes it became a very expensive affair to attend.

By Mark Graham

It was a bemused audience who after realising that the band were not going to play any more, filed out of the hall. Gratified for seeing what they had, but cheated out of their full quota.

Most of the songs, each lasting well under three minutes, were written by lead singer Paul Weller, who, at 19, is younger than some of his audience and well qualified to voice the frustrations of the punk generation.

Weller, together with bassist Bruce Foxton, mixed playing with acrobatic leaps and bounds across the stage.

Drummer Rick Buckler welded the songs together from his perch high at the back of the stage as the band swept through their hit singles In The City, All Around The World and the new album title track This Is The Modern World.

The rest flashed past in seconds and before most of the audience had chance to adjust to the frantic pogoing pace Jam had gone.

U.S TOUR

Before the concert the Jam told of their successful lightning tour of the States, but confessed to being glad to be back playing in front of British audiences.

"With us it is 50-50," said Bruce. "If the audience is enjoying themselves we enjoy ourselves."

There was no question of the 1,000-plus crowd not enjoying themselves; they could have kept on doing so for another half-hour at least. But the band did not play on.

BRUCE FOXTON of The Jam at the King's Hall last week.

© Alan Perry

49

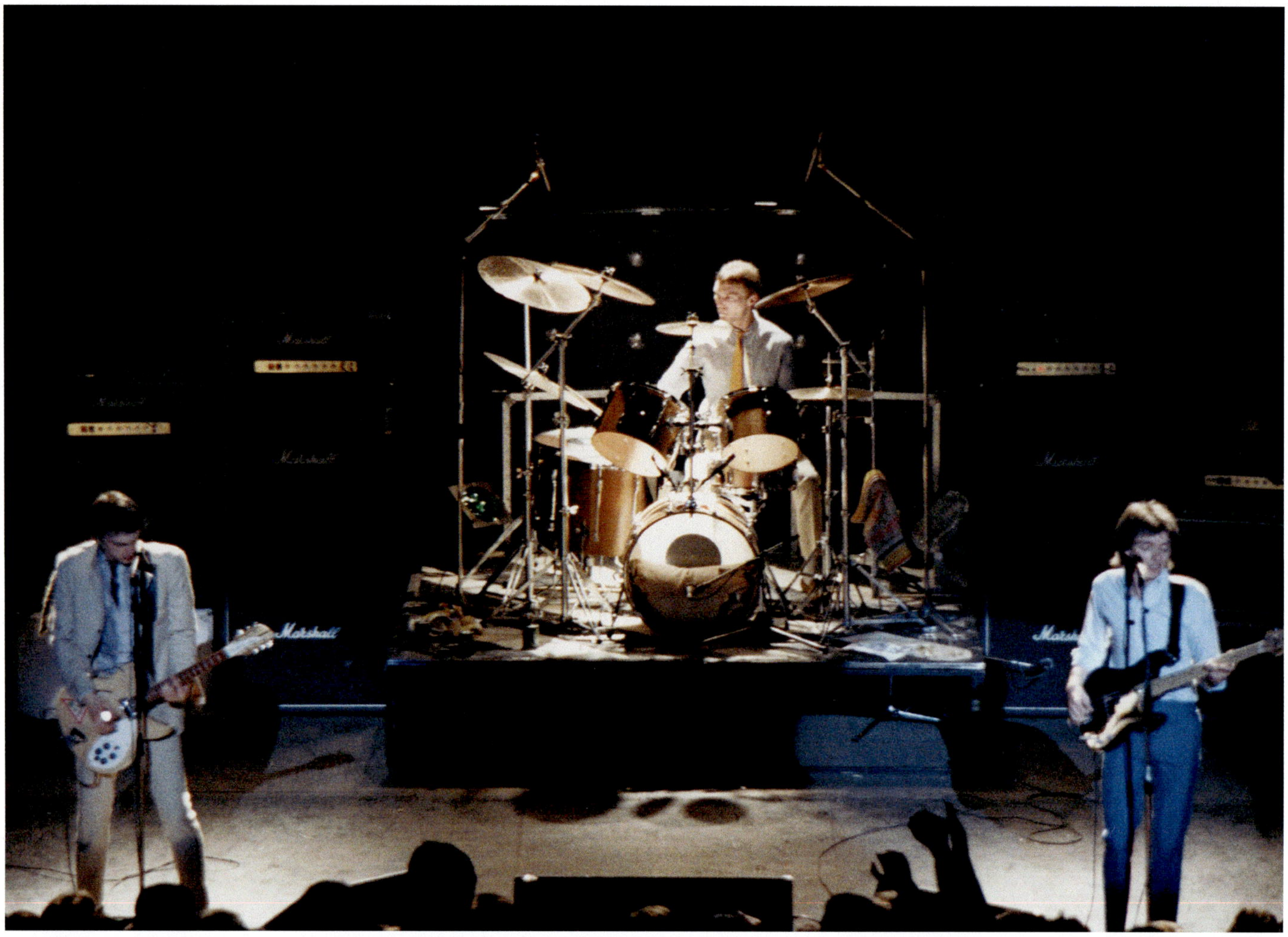

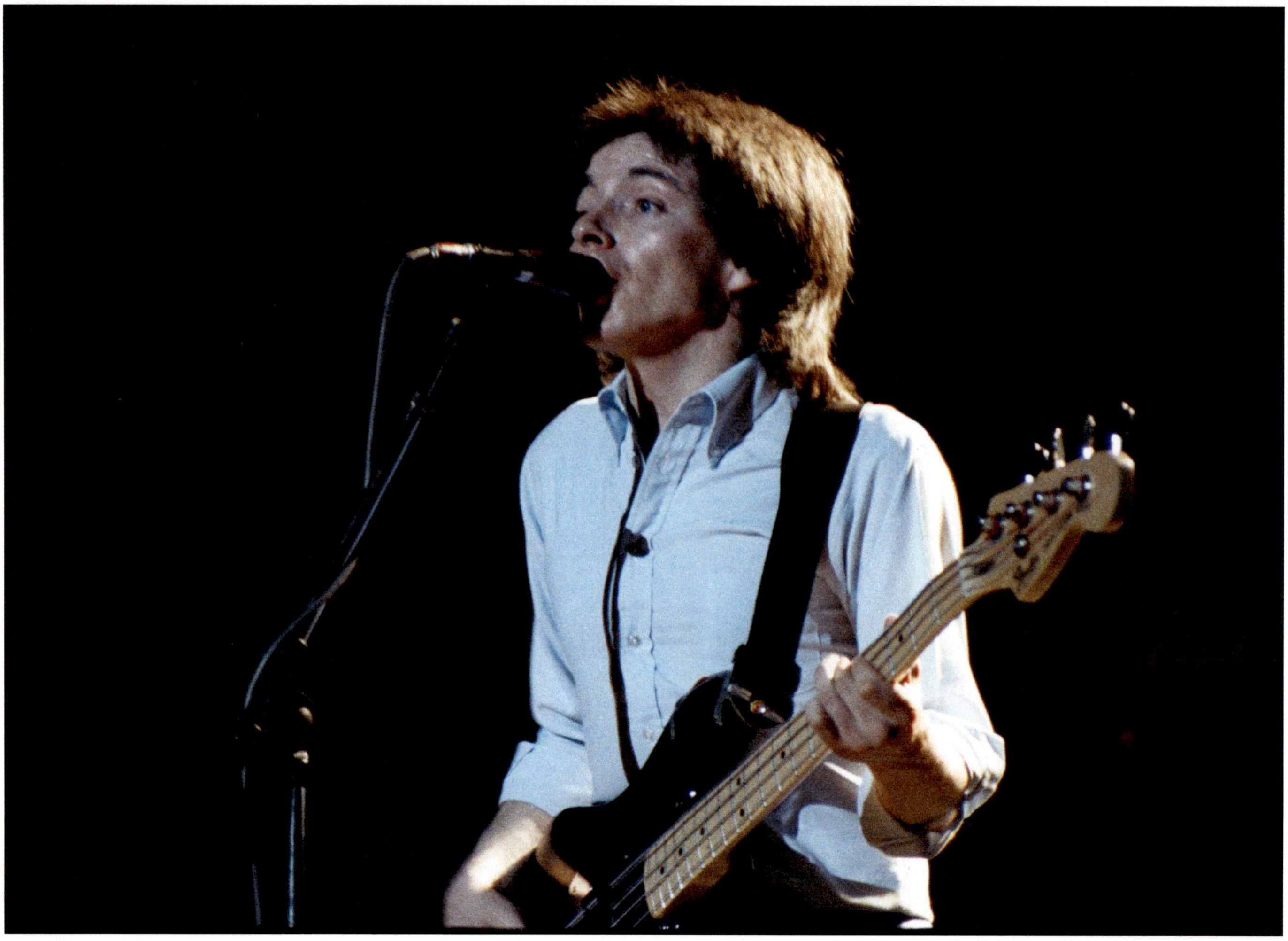

© Alan Perry

THE CLASH, BIRMINGHAM, 1977.

© Alan Perry

EVENING STANDARD, MONDAY, MAY 16, 1977—19

Back to Front

JAMES JOHNSON, in his report on the concert at the Rainbow Theatre [May 10], speaks of The Clash having become known as "the ultimate expression of an angry form of quasi-political nihilism."

What Mr Johnson did not report was vocalist Joe Strummer's statement on stage which made it clear to all who listened that he has no sympathies with the National Front and doesn't expect his fans to either.

This is what reporters such as Mr Johnson should repeat and emphasise rather than dwelling on exaggerated accounts of ripped seats.

Incidentally, it is surprising how very peaceful the concert was considering the provocative presence of far too many nervous and over-zealous security guards. — Beatrice Lass, Pangbourne Drive, Stanmore, Middlesex.

Back of a punk—but not a nihilist.

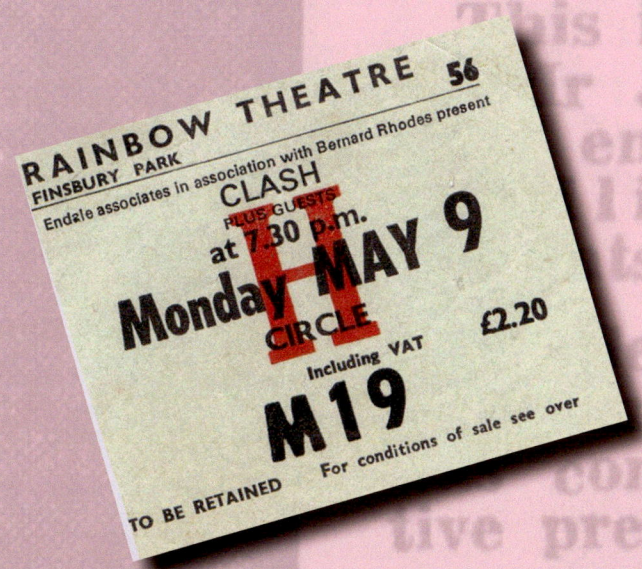

RAMONES, TOP RANK SUITE,
BIRMINGHAM, 28TH DECEMBER 1977

© Alan Perry

REZILLOS- AYLESBUR, 30TH DECEMBER 1977

REZILLOS
"Mission Accomplished . . .
But The Beat Goes On"
(WEA)

"Mission Accomplished ... But The Beat Goes On" is a fair summary of the Rezillos present situation. This farewell album, recorded live in their home town of Glasgow, is loud and fast moving, but tends to get boring after five or six tracks, when similarity between them is stretched to the limit.

The unmistakable warble of Fay Fife's voice is perhaps the reason why "Top Of The Pops" was such a hit and that is the best track on the album because of its varied sound and the excellent backing vocals by Gail Warning. The appreciative audience join in enthusiastically with "Somebody's Gonna Get Their Head Kicked In Tonite" and there are some good vocals by Eugene Reynolds on "Culture Shock."

We are told that although the Rezillos are dead, Fay and Eugene's ghosts will rock on with another "Rez" type group, but they won't have the same success, at least not with this repetitive sound.

© Alan Perry

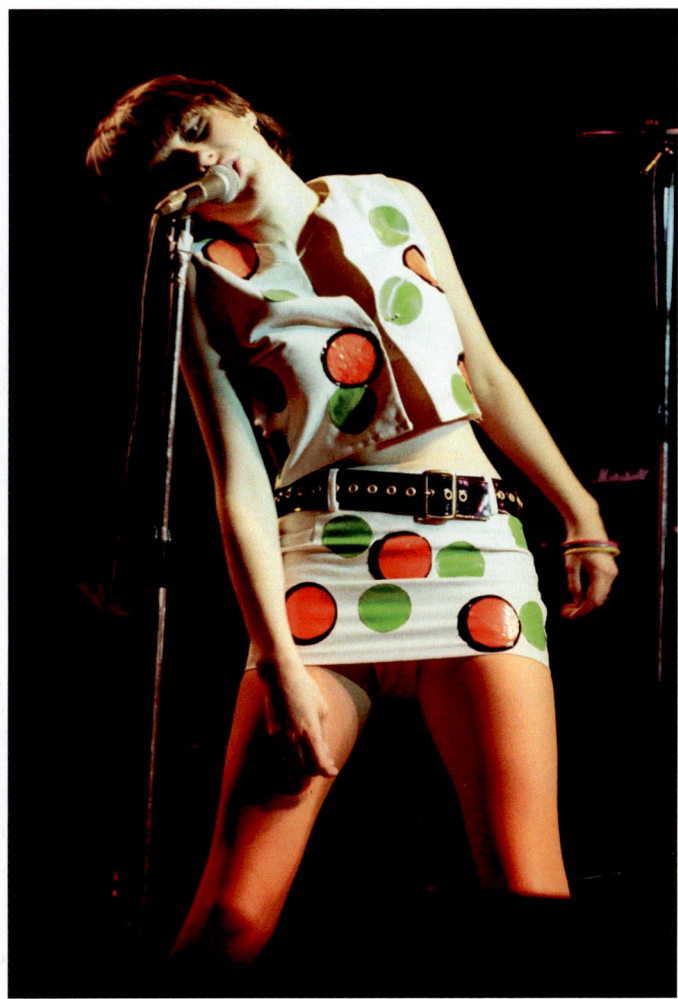

© Alan Perry

63

A BIGGS SINGLE — GOD SAVE THE SEX PISTOLS

VIRGIN RECORDS will rush release a new Sex Pistols single on June 16.

The single, a 12in, in a full colour sleeve will feature Ronald Biggs singing "God save the Sex Pistols" and Sid Vicious' rendering of "My Way".

Both tracks are from the soundtrack of the forthcoming Sex Pistols film.

Johnny Rotten is no longer involved with the Sex Pistols, and there seems to be no likelihood of a reconciliation. He will be recording with his new band as soon as circumstances permit, said a record company spokesman.

Vicious T-shirt anger

SEX PISTOLS manager Malcolm McLaren has been accused of cashing in on the stabbing death of Sid Vicious's girlfriend, Nancy Spungen.

McLaren faces criticism of some T-shirts which went on sale today at his King's Road boutique.

The T-shirts, at £6·50 each, show Vicious surrounded by a bunch of dead roses. Across the front are the words: "I'M ALIVE. SHE'S DEAD. I'M YOURS."

Vicious is currently in New York recovering from a suicide attempt after being charged with Spungen's murder.

Customers at the King's Road boutique said they found the T-shirt message tasteless.

George MacFarlane, bass guitarist with the New Wave band Grand Hotel, said: "I think it's really sick. It's just cashing in on Nancy's death."

ROCK

ACTRESS Toyah Willcox, who appeared in the film Jubilee, now moves into rock music with a new band at the ICA on Sunday night. Toyah is described as providing lead vocals and visual focus.

Never mind Sex Pistols ... pay £100

PUNK ROCK fan Terence Furnival saw red when the Sex Pistols were banned from appearing in Derby.

But his protest slogan on the pavement outside the Assembly Rooms in red paint was cut off in mid-sentence.

Two policemen pounced on him and were baffled when they read: "Never mind the leisure committee, what about . . ."

The mystery was solved at the police station, city magistrates heard yesterday. The complete version should have read: "Never mind the leisure committee, what about the Sex Pistols?" — imitating the group's LP record title: "Never mind the B———, here's the Sex Pistols."

Furnival (27), of Denbigh Street, Derby, pleaded guilty to damage and was fined £20, with £63 compensation, and £20 court costs.

He told the court: "I didn't write it for the sake of vandalism but to express a sincere point of view, of myself and lots of other people."

He had read in a newspaper the comment of the city entertainment manager that rock groups would not be allowed to play at the Rooms.

He had sent a letter in reply but it had not been published. Of the offence, he said: "It seemed a petty way to express my feelings but it was the only way I could."

But chairman of the bench Councillor Tom Taylor, told Furnival: "Derby is defaced enough as it is but to deface the slabs outside the Assembly Rooms is deplorable."

Mr Roger Exley, prosecuting, said Furnival was spotted by police and when arrested declared: "That's a bit petty isn't it?"

He told them: "The council banned the Sex Pistols from appearing in Derby and I wanted to protest about it."

WHEN THEY start calling it "trad punk," you know it's passed into history. my suspicions that the New Wave was all washed up were confirmed this week when I learnt that Rat Scabies, drummer of the now defunct punk group The Damned, has gone back to calling himself plain old Chris Miller. Now touring with a wholesomely English band called The White Cats, the ex - Rat explained blithely: "Rat Scabies became a bit silly, didn't it?" Yes.

Punk group storm off in TV rumpus

PUNK rock group The Stranglers stormed off stage during a BBC Television recording last night.

From the start of the concert at the University of Surrey in Guildford, they had shouted anti-student slogans to the audience.

After four numbers lead guitarist Hugh Cornwell threw a microphone and stand across the stage shouting: "We don't like playing to an elitist audience."

Then bass guitarist Jean Jacques Burnel threw himself across the drum kit, smashing it.

At this point the group ran off stage.

A National Union of Students organiser walked on stage and announced that they would try to get the group back on later.

BBC producer Michael Appleton said: "The band are not going to come back because I don't want them to come back."

Jean Jacques Burnel said the band had no intention of coming back anyway.

He described what they had just done as "commercial suicide.

"I suppose we get sued by the BBC," he said. "We happen to enjoy playing gigs but to fans who buy our records — not just students."

He said the students had got advantages that others hadn't and were conservative and reactionary.

Mr. Appleton said: "This came as much as a surprise to me as to everyone else. It has been a waste of time."

He said he might transmit some of the recording but only to ridicule the group.

The BBC had been at the University of Surrey, recording a programme in the series Rock Goes to College.

The Stranglers . . . Hugh Cornwell, Dave Greenfield, Jet Black and Jean Jacques Burnel

EVENING STANDARD, FRIDAY, JANUARY 6, 1978—3

SUBDUED DEBUT—the Sex Pistols in action in Atlanta, Georgia—Sid Vicious on bass, lead singer Johnny Rotten, and, right, lead guitarist Steve Jones.

Rotten and Co. 'run of the mill'

NEWS ON CAMERA

From David Douglas

ATLANTA
VICE SQUAD detectives from the Bible Belt of the United States gave the Sex Pistols their blessing after the first night of the group's American tour.

The band hit Atlanta, Georgia, with all the force of a limp pop gun.

Atlanta's tiny punk community turned up in force—about five of them — dressed in shredded T-shirts held together by safety-pins, but most of the audience were blue-jeaned college students who wouldn't have looked out of place at a square dance.

And the Pistols, who appeared in what is normally a folk club, were sent up by the university group who preceded them. They had opened with a singer impaled by 4ft. safety pins.

Widespread publicity had police scurrying from across American to see the Sex Pistols. But it seems they are no threat to the Great American Way of Life.

Lieutenant. R. B. Howell of the police department in Memphis, Tennessee, said : "They were a run-of-the-mill band and I don't reckon they'll be a problem. And I didn't hear them swear."

The mild reaction may have been due to language difficulties.

As one Atlanta police officer said: "I didn't catch any four-letter words but with that English accent I only caught about four words."

The band, whose album, Never Mind the Bollocks, Here's the Sex Pistols, is standing at No 108 on the Billboard US Charts, packed the tiny 550-seat Great Southeast Music Hall, but hardly raised the roof.

The atmosphere was electric but far from violent. Singer Johnny Rotten wiped his nose with his sleeve, coughed freely, cursed frequently and jerked around like a maniacal puppet.

Ian Tomlinson, 17, of Haywards Heath, on holiday in the United States, drove nearly 200 miles from Birmingham, Alabama, just to take in the show.

"They were good, but they were quiet," he said.

Paul Miller, 22, an engineering student, said: "It was good. I liked it, but I don't see weirdos like that making it big over here. It was odd but an interesting experience."

They may do better at their next two stops, Memphis, Tennessee, and Baton Rouge, Louisana, but so far the Sex Pistols have confused rather than excited or enraged the Americans.

● Nine Finish youth organisations have appealed to the Ministry of the Interior to stop the Sex Pistols from appearing in Helsinki on January 18 because of their " sick mass culture directed at youngsters and children."

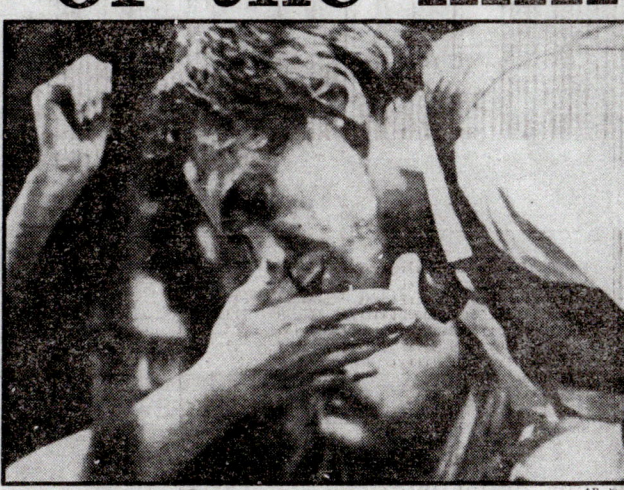

A PAT on the cheek from a fan in Atlanta last night for Sex Pistols singer Johnny Rotten.

WHAT HAPPENS AT A...

PUNK war has been joined between Malcolm McLaren, currently preparing his film about the brief life and times of the Sex Pistols, and the makers of the cultish Punk Rock Movie.

PRM, made by disc-jockey Don Letts, was shown in 8mm at the ICA last year and then, in 35mm, commerical cinema size, had some success in the U.S.

Now producer Peter Clifton wants to release it in British cinemas.

But McLaren, who uses the song in his own film, is refusing to give him the rights to the Pistols' God Save The Queen — with which the defunct group open and close the movie.

"This has prevented us from releasing the film here," says Clifton, who has permission from Johnny Rotten and Sid Vicious (but not the other members of the group, Paul Cook or Steve Jones) to use the punk anthem.

"We've had clearances from all the other groups in the picture."

Says John Tiberi from McLaren's company Glitterbest: "Before you use a song, you have to pay for the rights. All Malcolm wants to do is have a chance to make his own statement about the Sex Pistols before Peter Clifton jumps on the bandwagon."

BOOMTOWN RATS, BARBARELLA'S, BIRMINGHAM, FEBRUARY 1978

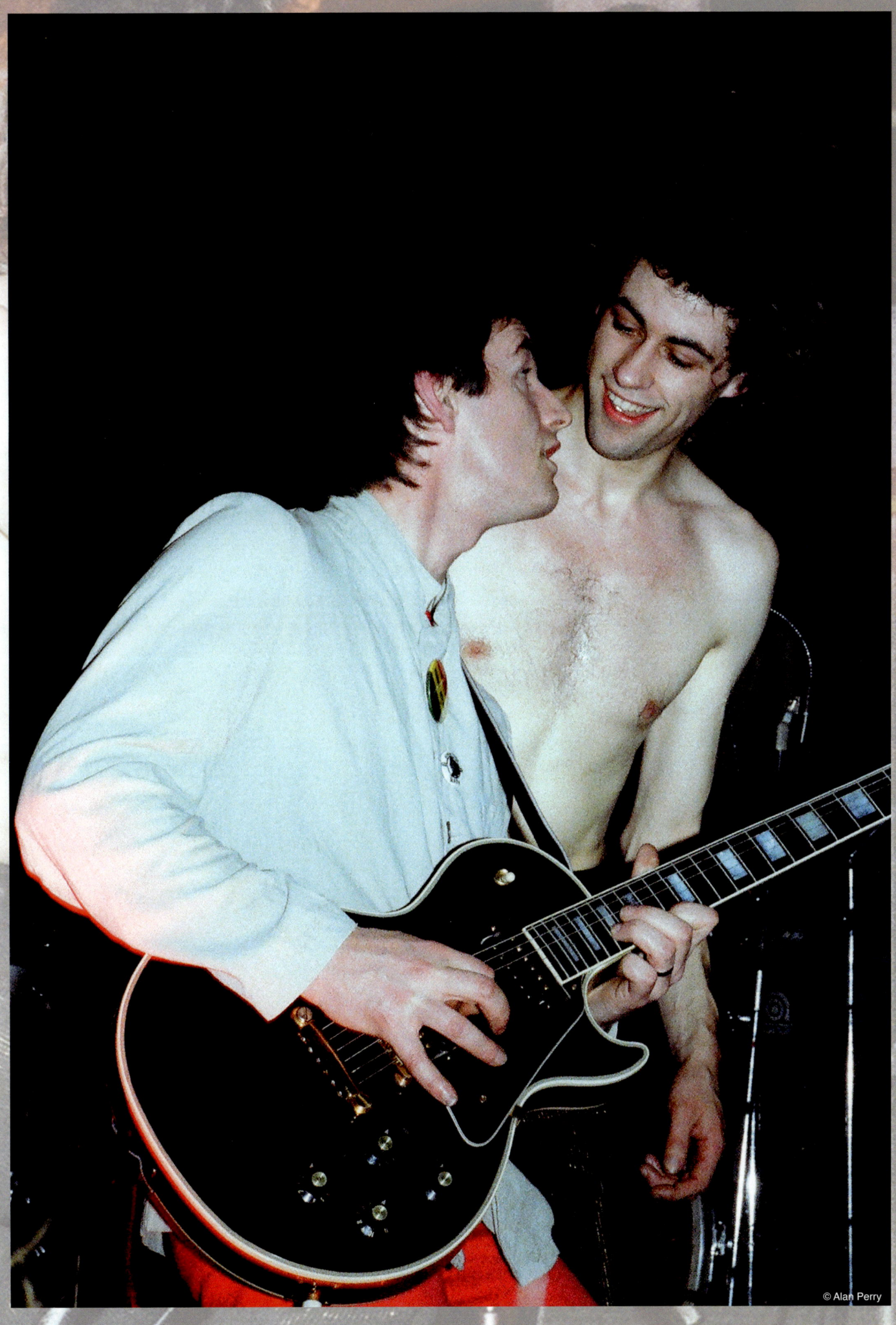

68

© Alan Perry

© Alan Perry

69

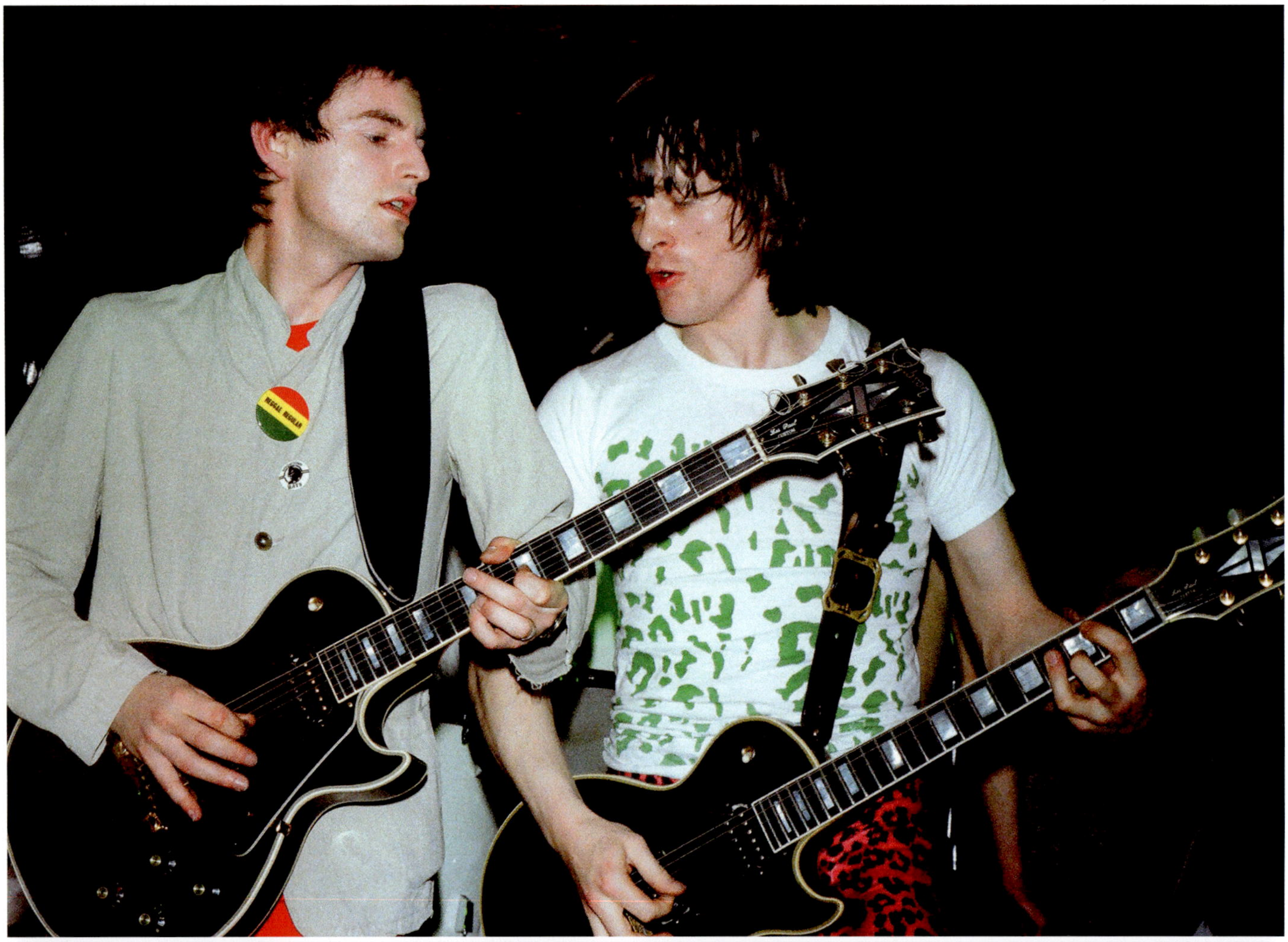

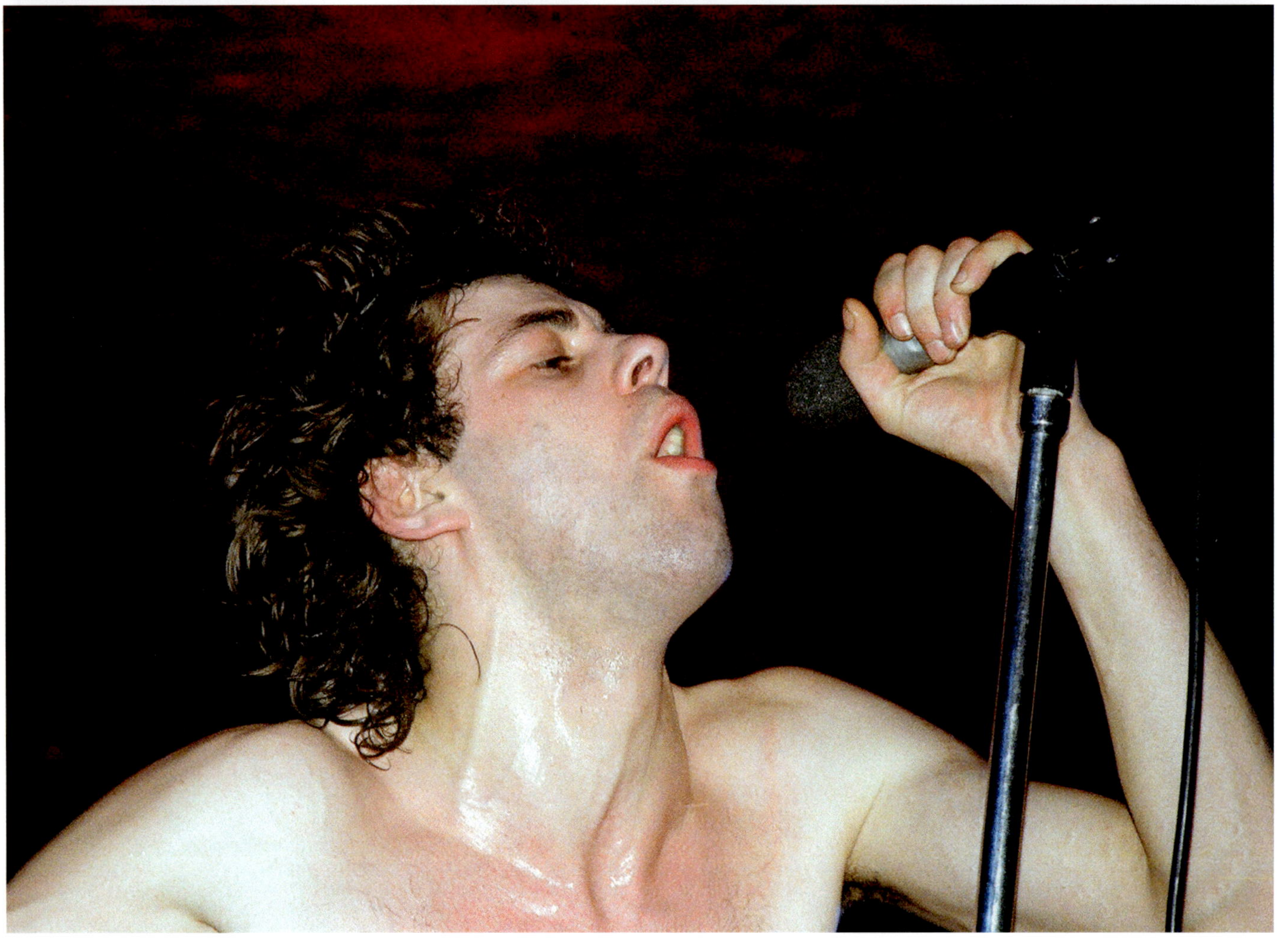

Carnival of the Left-footed jackboots

ON Sunday Mr Benn meets the punks. The occasion of this decidedly strange encounter is the second national Carnival organised by the increasingly active Anti-Nazi League. It is the follow-up to a similar event held last April, which attracted some 80,000 people ranging from the committed members of extreme Left-wing groups to the rebellious but politically unsophisticated devotees of punk rock.

With that same blend of politics and pop the promoters of "Carnival Two" are talking in terms of bringing 100,000 demonstrators on to the streets of London. After a rally in Hyde Park they will march across the river to a rock concert at a park in Brixton.

At the rally, Labour's own Tony Benn heads a list of speakers who clearly reflect the political orientation of the Anti-Nazi League. There is Arthur Scargill, the Yorkshire miners' leader; Bill Keys, the Left-wing general secretary of the Society of Graphical and Allied Trades and chairman of the TUC Equal Rights Committee; and Paul Holborrow, the Socialist Workers' party member who is the league's full-time secretary. At the musical end, assorted punk and black reggae groups are to appear.

It remains to be seen just how many people respond to the ANL's call, how many of the pop fans will bother themselves with the preliminaries in Hyde Park, and indeed whether the star speakers join in the fun at Brixton. But the Anti-Nazi League is convinced that the mixture is a winning formula, that will enable it to put its message across to a large, young audience and to begin to indoctrinate some youngsters into taking part in concerted, politically conscious activity in the future.

This approach is one of a number of ways in which the Anti-Nazi campaign has built itself up in the past 10 months into a skilful propaganda machine. Since its inception last November the ANL claims to have recruited 30,000 followers in 250 branches, with an additional 150 national sponsors, public figures including over 30 Labour MPs, academics, stage personalities, journalists, writers and sportsmen. Not all of these celebrities are by any means Left-wing activists, and few appear to contribute positively to the ANL's work.

A dozen trade unions have affiliated to the league, at least one of which, the Civil and Public Services Association, has given it financial assistance. Another source of funds is the Rowntree Trust, which in the league's earliest days gave it a grant of £2,400.

Despite the moral worthiness of its aims—publicly to oppose the racialism of the National Front — and its claim that it is non-party political, the ANL is first and last an extreme Left-wing campaign. It is the vehicle of those who wish to inflame emotions and exploit tensions in society. Anyone who is seriously concerned to promote racial harmony in Britain should be alarmed by the degree to which such bodies, dedicated to conflict and disruption, have been able to turn the issue of race to their own advantage, to mislead some sections of liberal opinion and to prey upon the fears of minority groups.

The idea for a broad anti-NF campaign came from the Socialist Workers' party in the wake of last summer's riots at Lewisham and elsewhere, in which its members had played a violent role. The SWP approached individual members of the Labour Left, who responded enthusiastically. An unholy alliance was forged. Full-time workers and the nucleus of active members were provided by the Socialist Workers, who in their monthly journal maintained that "the Anti-Nazi League can create a massive new audience for revolutionary socialism. It can offer a positive way of fighting the system to angry and cynical young people."

After initial reserve, the Communist party joined in, hailing the

EDWARD SHIPLEY
on the reality behind Anti-Nazi League events in London this weekend

campaign as an example of "what the broad democratic alliance, central to Communist party strategy, is all about." Also actively involved in the ANL is the Trotskyist International Marxist Group, which the report of Lord Justice Scarman held responsible for violence at an anti-NF demonstration in Red Lion Square in 1974.

Since that early violent clash, the theme of "smashing the Nazis" has grown to become during the past 12 months an obsession with the Far Left. At a time when traditional areas of activity, such as trade unions, have been relatively quiescent, militants have sunk all their energies into anti-racialist campaigns. The ANL has not been the only one, but it is the largest and most wide ranging.

Affiliated to the league are innumerable sub-groups catering for minorities and special interests. Most are predictable and have been established among existing circles of activists. Among them is a Student Campaign Against the Nazis, Schoolkids Against the Nazis, and there are "Against the Nazis" groups for women, trade unionists, media workers, teachers, civil servants, vegetarians, Spurs supporters and "Gays." There is relatively little support among immigrant communities.

Setting aside the more ludicrous examples, the ANL's insidious totalitarianism is best illustrated by its campaign in the media to "pull the plug" on any party political broadcasts that may be made by the National Front and to prevent all reporting of the Front which does not "expose" its activities. But this blantant censorship by direct action could prove counter-productive. Instead of giving an intelligent electorate the opportunity to hear for itself just how objectionable the NF is, censorship would be more likely to give the Front cause for complaint, and enable it to plead for support from a public purposely kept in ignorance or fed with Leftist propaganda. And once begun, "pulling the plug" would all too easily extend to other parties on race or other issues.

The justification offered for the launching of the Anti-Nazi League was that the influence of the National Front was increasing. This remains the underlying assumption of the league's present activities. It would be more objective to say that all the evidence suggests that the NF is in retreat. The decline in its electoral performance began at the local elections in May 1977, in areas such as Leicester, the West Midlands or Yorkshire where the Front considered itself strongest.

By-elections have produced generally bad results for a year now and this year's local election results were a disaster. The ANL can take some credit for this but by no means all, since the process began before it appeared on the scene. In addition, churchmen, politicians of all parties and the media have spoken out against the National Front. And public awareness that the ideology of NF leaders is directly inspired by German Nazism, including a barely concealed anti-semitism and latent violence, has been growing for some time.

The ANL's main contribution has been the dubious one of confronting the NF on the streets, and by the militant threats from its own supporters forcing the authorities to invoke the Public Order Act to ban marches.

But an emotive movement like the Anti-Nazi League constantly needs new issues to maintain its momentum and preserve its somewhat uncertain unity. The ANL is planning a major propaganda intervention in the General Election, in which its main aim will be to prevent the loss of Labour votes in working-class constituencies on racial issues. It will do this not only by opposing the NF but by smearing Tories with the "racialist" tag. The faster the NF threat fades, the more the emphasis will turn on alleged racialism in the Conservative party as the greater evil.

The Left does not have nor should it be allowed to have a monopoly of moral opposition to racialism. The Federation of Conservative Students sought to demonstrate this fact when it affiliated to the ANL. But it soon realised the way to bring about a harmonious society is not by revolutionary agitation and distorting facts in favour of the Labour party.

Detectives hired for Vicious defence case

Private investigators have been hired to help punk star Sid Vicious, accused of killing his girl-friend in a New York hotel.

Mr. Malcolm McLaren, former manager of the Sex Pistols, said yesterday: "We are using private detectives to present the best possible defence case."

Vicious, (21), is in a jail drug clinic receiving treatment for heroin addiction.

Mr. McLaren said in New York: "I should know tomorrow whether I have raised the £25,000 needed for Sid's bail.

"However, I want to talk to Sid himself and his doctors before deciding whether it might be best to leave him in the clinic.

"But he will be going back to the notoriously tough Riker's Island prison at the end of the week, and I'm determined to stop that happening."

Vicious — real name John Ritchie — is accused of murdering Miss Nancy Spungen, his former go-go dancer girlfriend, aged 20.

Anti-Nazi League is Marxist—Front chief

THE Anti-Nazi League, established to fight the right-wing National Front, is dominated by Marxist revolutionaries working to establish a Communist dictatorship in Britain, the Front say in a 24-page booklet published today.

The Front claim that by the use of famous personalities, the League falsely gives the public the impression of being peaceful, lawful and non-political.

But in an open letter to sponsors of the League, Front president Squadron Leader John Harrison-Broadley says: "Despite its pretentions to moderation and non-violence, the Anti-Nazi League is patently a front for rampant Marxism and a launching platform for hysterical violence."

The report is edited by National Front activities officer Mr. Martin Webster. Called "Lifting the lid off the Anti-Nazi League," it is to be circulated to Members of Parliament, local councillors, libraries, schools, and to the police.

'TRICKED'

In his open letter, Squadron Leader Harrison-Broadley says: "The real purpose of the Anti-Nazi League is not even primarily to combat the National Front, but to advance the power of Marxist revolutionaries who control the Anti-Nazi League at all levels.

"Their objectives are threefold: 1, to build a 'Popular Front' embracing the Labour Party and the extreme left, and thereby to unite their forces in a more powerful and effective alliance; 2, to recruit new converts to their ranks; and 3, to prepare the way for violent revolution by inuring their young supporters to violence, first against the National Front, then against the police, and finally against society as a whole."

The National Front president says that through its use of sports personalities, showbiz celebrities and others the League "tries to give the general public the impression that it is a peaceful, lawful, constitutional non-party political and above all respectable pressure group devoted to maintaining freedom and democracy — even the British way of life!

"If you have this impression of the Anti-Nazi League, you have been tricked. The Anti-Nazi League is a vicious, violent, and subversive alliance of Marxist opportunists, self-publicists, and agitators."

PISTOLS MANAGER FLIES TO SEE SID

SEX PISTOLS' manager Malcolm McLaren flew to New York today as group member Sid Vicious was to appear in court accused of knifing to death his go-go dancer girlfriend Nancy Sungen.

He was expected to arrive in New York probably after 21-year-old Vicious's morning court appearance.

At Mr. McLaren's London office, his secretary said: "We just don't know what is happening at the moment. Malcolm has gone over to try and sort everything out."

Mr. McLaren said on leaving Heathrow: "Sid had tremendous outbursts of temper, but I can't bring myself to believe that Sid would even contemplate doing anything like this."

Vicious, bass guitarist for the Sex Pistols until he broke away from the controversial Punk group earlier this year, was arrested on a murder charge yesterday after the body of 20-year-old Nancy Spungen was found at the Chelsea Hotel where they had been staying for three weeks.

Vicious, aged 21, was charged under his real name of John Simon Ritchie.

THE STRANGLERS, LONDON, BATTERSEA PARK, 16TH SEPTEMBER, 1978.

© Alan Perry

© Alan Perry

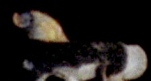

© Alan Perry

BURNEL'S LONDON GIG STRANGLED

THE prestigious London debut of Jean Jacques Burnel's solo band and a large chunk of The Pop Group's first main tour have been cancelled — because both acts overestimated public response to their music.

Burnel was due to play at London's Hammersmith Odeon on Tuesday this week, but late last week the show was mysteriously cancelled, or "postponed", until a future date. This marks the second big problem for Burnel over playing in London, as his first choice of venue, the Theatre Royal in Drury Lane, cancelled the booking when they realised the star was a Strangler.

The London concert was to be the last date of his Euroman tour, which has been attracting less than capacity audiences at most of the shows, and the promoters have said that the show has been "postponed" for about three weeks.

London's Harlesden New Roxy was pencilled in as an alternative venue for Saturday this week, but the promoters decided not to take up their option. The only reason given was that Burnel "was not happy with the idea of closing the tour at Hammersmith" — he wasn't ready for it," and plans are going ahead to try and rebook a date in London soon after the Stranglers have appeared at the Loch Lomond Festival at the end of the month.

● The Pop Group, who set out on an ambitious tour of large British halls on Friday last week to try to push their debut Radar album, "Y," have pulled out of ten of the 17 shows and are rearranging the tour.

The band have retained their booking at London's Leicester Square Empire Ballroom on May 7, but rearranged large chunks of the rest of the tour, cancelling concerts at Bristol, Newcastle, Liverpool, Manchester, Loughborough, Edinburgh, Malvern, Chelmsford, Norwich and Guildford.

Some of the concerts have been rescheduled, and the new tour list, following London, is: Aberdeen University (May 11), St Andrews University (13), Southampton University (16), Liverpool University (18), Manchester University (19), Bristol University (21), and Newcastle Poly (26).

The band were originally advised to play smaller clubs on the tour, which was set up primarily to increase album sales, but they insisted on going for universities, which are notoriously poor for boosting sales. When a general lack of response from the venues on the tour became evident last week, the group agreed that the dates should be re-booked.

Extra support groups Dambala and Exodus have now pulled out of the tour, and The Pop Group will be supported by the Good Missionaries only.

JEAN JACQUES

THE POP GROUP . . . in the cold?

Cornwell's solo

HUGH CORNWELL, shortly to join his fellow Stranglers for their headline appearance at the Loch Lomond Festival at the end of May, is putting the finishing touches to his debut solo album.

The record, "Nosferatu", was named after the first Dracula movie, and is planned for release in June. Cornwell has just returned from America's West Coast, where he has been recording the album with a number of players, including former Mother of Invention Ian Underwood, and Captain Beefheart's drummer, Robert Williams.

CORRIGANS RECORDS
15 Grimsby Road,
Cleethorpes.
Telephone 40703.

BIG ROCK POSTERS
IN COLOUR.

Buzzcock, Bowie, Penetration, Johnny Rotton, Banshees, Kiss, BLondie, Boomtown Rats, Clash, Billy Idol, Gaye Advert, Ian Dury, Stranglers, Devo, Jimmy Pursey, Elvis, Yes, Queen, Status Quo.

Don't miss out,,
see for yourself

Schoolboy editor aims at New Wave fans
By Sylvia Collier

Stephen Marshall is one of London's youngest magazine editors — at 15 he is the founder of a new music magazine launched for fans of the New Wave.

Stephen, who goes to Chelsea School, has lost no time in achieving what many youngsters dream about — starting his own paper. And it was his teachers at school who helped the idea take shape.

"At the end of last year I had just been to hear the Ramones and was talking about it to my English teacher at school. He said 'Why don't you do a review.' That started me off," said Stephen. "I was typing it out and I thought why don't I do more, and get a magazine going. So I did."

Issue number one took shape fairly quickly. "A girl I know did a drawing of Joey from the Ramones for the front. It was just one page, back and front, which I gave away. Everyone liked it so I thought I'd do another."

The magazine was called "Raw Power", after an album title Stephen liked, and issue number two came out packed with reviews of concerts, local gigs, and records.

Encouragement for the project came from Chelsea School's music resources officer and interest gathered amongst Stephen's friends. "Now I have a few more people to help. A mate of mine, and I are going to go to photography classes together. We hope to make the magazine a lot better."

But Stephen plans to wait for a few months before really devoting a lot of energy to the magazine — he is now studying at school to take C.S.E. and G.C.E. examinations, soon in English, biology, maths, environmental science and art.

Later, his ambition is to become a professional journalist with the music press. "It's what I enjoy doing," says Stephen.

● Extract from a page review of a Hammersmith Odeon show last November.

It's hard to get people going in this place.
The Banshees are much more suited to all standing venues.
They push through the set.
Thier stage act as cold as thier music.
Siouxsie
Almost devoid of emotion.
Wearing familiar Umbro shorts over black trousers.
Moves initialisingly around the enormous stage.
"I don't want to ruin my microphone, so pack it in!"
Some one had obviously tried to grab hold of her.
She turns away and continues with the show.
Her wiry body springing up and down the catwalk.
Motivating the audience to limited movement.
Only one encore
and its all over.
A comment from a girl next to me was,
"Sham 69 £1.50 and they were on all night?
This set was short , too short
Can't understand any.

Album review

Scared to Dance, the title track of the Skids' album and also released on Virgin as a single, is an anthem of shy and fallible youth.

Dossier, the next track, is a slightly more sensitive version of the same but Richard Jobson, Skids vocals and guitar, belts out the two as one and drowns a lot of good music.

The album could be very good if it would, for a moment, give us a break from the repetitive dirge of Mr Jobson's delivery.

Charles, by lead and rhythm guitarist Stuart Adamson, is a short, sharp and ruthless number which seems to have escaped the rough treatment, and William Simpson on bass and Thomas Kellichan on drums almost make the album worth buying. Better stick to the single.

Skids — Days in Europe (Virgin). This new wave band works with big themes. Richard Jobson, singer and songwriter of the band, has calmly tackled the subject of war on this second album and Stuart Adamson has worked the theme into several memorable tunes, often delivered as driving dance music or wrapped in the big sound of Bill Nelson's keyboard work. Confident and classy.

I APPROACHED "Scared to Dance" (Virgin) by the Scottish group the Skids with caution. Could it be another album of repetitive, meaningless words from a fading punk scene? Far from it. It is a fast-moving, hard-hitting sound from a group who have had little recognition so far — something this record will change.

Although there is a military trend throughout the album, each song is different with imaginative lyrics and interesting combinations of instruments and chords. Included in the album is "Into the Valley", their latest hit single, a good illustration of their work.

Lead singer 18-year-old Richard Jobson has a strong voice, although occasionally the lyrics are hard to distinguish. The album has punk characteristics but the Skids deny that they are a punk group. They say they have only borrowed the image and style, not the music or lyrics.

One track is especially good — "Dossier (Of Fallibility)", which has a haunting melody and a catchy verse. The Skids, say their agent, "are skidding forwards". I couldn't agree more.

LEICESTER MERCURY, WEDNESDAY, OCTOBER 17, 1979

PERSONALITY PLUS POWER SHOWS WHY BOB IS KING RAT

critics critics critics

THE SHEER POWER and personality of Bob Geldof made certain that last night's concert by The Boomtown Rats turned out to be the rock event of the year in Leicester.

In the steamy heat of the packed Granby Halls, lead singer Geldof dominated the concert so effectively that the rest of the Irish band seemed almost incidental.

ROCK

Everything Geldof did was dramatic and unexpected — arms pumping, running furiously on the spot one moment, then clambering around the stage scaffolding the next.

Still the Rats do have another talent — the well-named Johnny Fingers on keyboards. When Geldof ducked from the spotlight it was Johnny who caught the eye with his striped pyjamas, and ear with his brilliant playing.

All the favourite hits and album tracks were there for the fans to savour with Rat Trap and I Don't Like Mondays taking Pride of place. But for me the highlight was Joey's on the Street Again with some cool saxophone thrown in.

Geldof was visibly annoyed that the sound wasn't spot on. But it failed to mar the show

And after acknowledging the deafening cheers of 'more' at the end, he joked: "Perhaps we will come here next time after all."

Superb lighting effects with an extraordinary nought and crosses framework towering over the stage, added spice to a generally outstanding concert.

But my main memory of the concert will be the non-stop activity of Bob Geldof, the bionic man of rock. He resembled a human windmill at times — well it was one way of keeping cool in the balmy atmosphere.

Mick Jagger may have been the rock concert hero of the 60s and 70s but Geldof looks set to take over his mantle in the 1980s.

— David Watson

Bob Geldof at the Granby Halls, Leicester, last night.

'Band that can't play' recipe for punk group

THE script for planned film featuring the controversial Sex Pistols, gave a lesson in manufacturing a punk rock group, Mr Justice BROWNE-WILKINSON was told in the High Court yesterday.

It said: "Find yourself four kids. Make them hate each other. Make sure they can't play.

The group's manager, MALCOLM McLAREN, was scripted as saying: "The main asset is a band that can't play. Cash comes out of chaos."

JOHNNY ROTTEN, the group's lead singer, is suing Mr McLaren's management company, Glitterbest, under his real name, JOHN LYDON, following the break-up of the Sex Pistols last year. He is asking the judge to appoint a receiver to collect and preserve money for members of the disbanded group.

The 29-page script also referred to making newspaper headlines by shouting about incest, drugs and necrophilia.

It contained references to Jack the Ripper, the Moors murderess Myra Hindley, and the Cambridge rapist, said Mr JOHN WILMERS, Q C, representing Lydon.

It referred to Mr McLaren saying that he found John Lydon lurking in a shop corner. "Had it not been for his green hair I would have taken him for Micawber's clerk."

Scene with train robber

The planned film also had scenes of the train robber Ronald Biggs, featured with the group and the script contained the phrase: "Cosh the driver. Belsen was a gas."

In written evidence, the 22-year-old singer said Mr Maclaren was not interested in the group's music but only in publicity.

He felt strongly for the group's music and the need for regular live appearances, but throughout 1977 Mr McLaren said he was unable to arrange any.

The case was adjourned until today.

★ ★ ★

THE CLASH seem to attract the strangest people.

At their recent Lyceum gig a naked girl leapt onto the stage and tried to molest singer Joe Strummer. She was immediately thrown back by a willing bodyguard.

Now, boys, that's no way to treat a lady . . .

LENE LOVICH, BIRMINGHAM ODEON
22ND OCTOBER 1979

Stunning concert by Lene Lovich

LENE LOVICH'S gig at Loughborough University on Saturday night had a distinctive cosmopolitan flavour. It was also a presentation of stark visual contrasts.

American-born Lene, the daughter of a Yugoslavian father and an English mother, emerged on stage wearing a dark purple and bright yellow costume of silk, lace and leather rounded off with a pair of gipsy earrings and two-foot long pigtails.

The music was slightly Gothic with snatches of Egyptian melodies and Eastern European marches and chants thrown in.

She danced jerkily, something like a punk Kate Bush deprived of Lindsay Kemp's mime tuition, through an exciting set which was lapped up by a frenzied student audience.

But of course it was Lene's remarkable voice which was the main feature of the act. It is a voice of extraordinary variety, both in tone and range and it brought her fame earlier this year with the hit single Lucky Number.

Another hit, Say When, followed and now, in the wake of European tour and midway through her second major British tour, her latest single Bird Song looks set to bring Lene more thoroughly deserved success.

The gig was backed by the superb and beautiful Jane Aire from the U.S.A. and Dutch band The Meteors.

And if all that wasn't enough Lene even had a little philosophy for the audience: "Be brave and strong and follow your heart, but don't hurt anybody please."

Sounds like good advice from this stunningly attractive and talented lady.

—Duncan Hopwood

Russian ahead of the rest

**Lene Lovich,
Odeon, New Street, B'ham.**

SHE looks like a cross between Grann's Angel and a gypsy from the steppes of Russia.

She believes in reincarnation and professes to having no home.

Bizarre she may be but Lene Lovich is a success.

The songs are strident new wave with an infectious Slavonic, Romany rhythm.

Her voice is an elastic band, bending and stretching and warping notes.

The set was a mixture of old songs (One In a Million, Say When, Lucky Number) and new (the magical Birdsong, The Angels, You Can't Kill Me, What Would I Do Without You) but a highlight was a highly individual version of the Four Season's classic The Night.

I loved it.

She was supported by Jane Aire and the Belvederes, featuring a little lady with a big voice who will make it with the right material, and The Meteors, who seemed to deserve their place in the billing.

TOM REID

THE UNDERTONES AT THE MARQUEE, LONDON, 1979

JAKE BURNS, STIFF LITTLE FINGERS, 1979

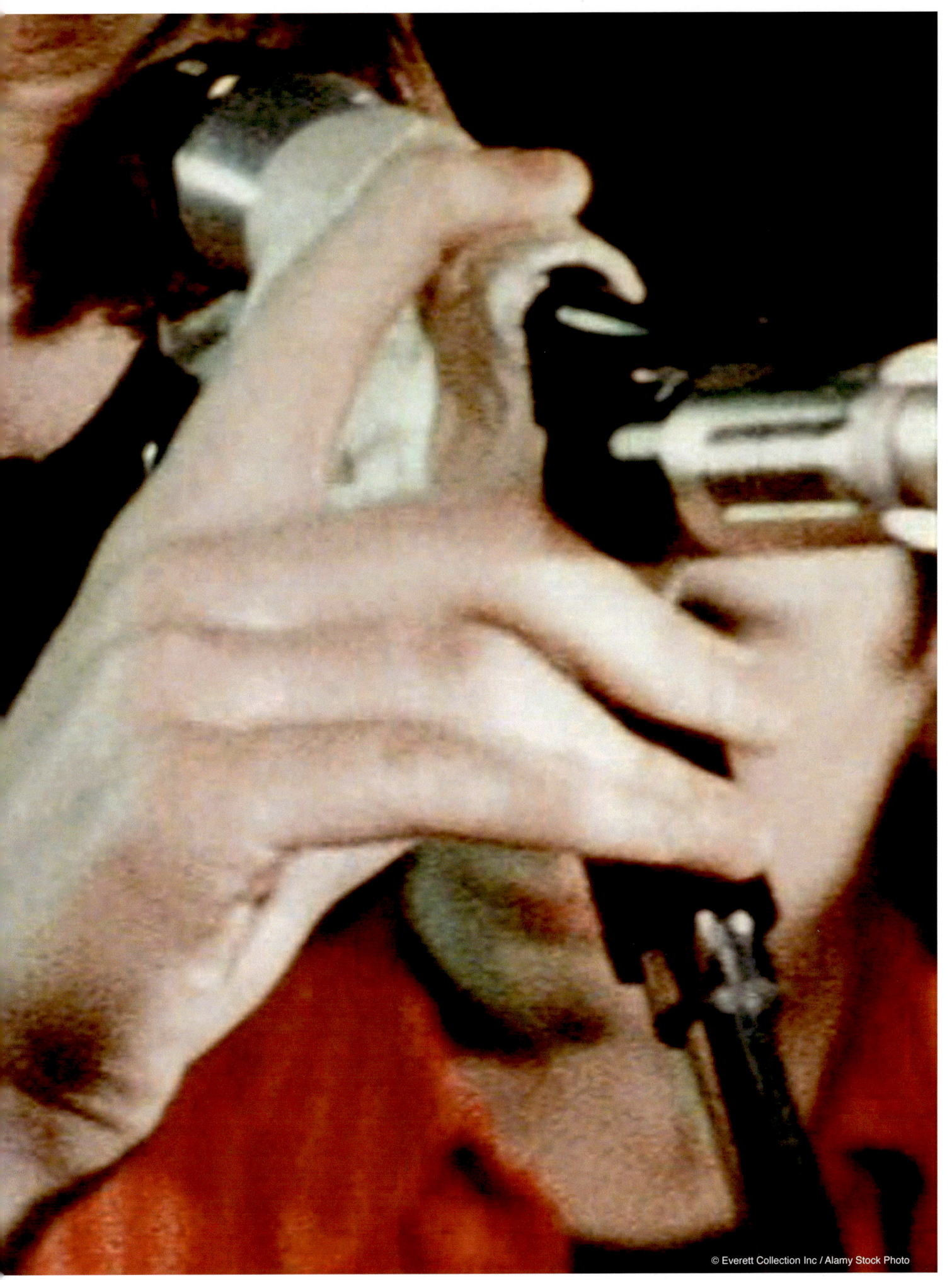

UK SUBS, FROM LEFT: CHARLIE HARPER, PETE DAVIES AND NICK GARRATT, 14TH SEPTEMBER 1979.

Solo sub

THE UK SUBS, who've been without a label since the sudden demise of Gem Records, are in the final stages of negotiating a new deal, which they hope to announce next week.

Meanwhile, **Charlie Harper** releases his second solo single next weekend on Ramkup Records (through Pinnacle). Called 'Freaked', it consists of Charlie and "a bunch of old cronies (but not as old as Charlie)" made up of **Tony Collins** guitar, **Steve Slack** bass, **Dave Dudley** keyboards and **Pete Davies** drums.

Men in black back again

THE STRANGLERS (above) have emerged from a period of management and legal hassles to set up a 20-date tour in February.

The band release a new single on Liberty Records on January 19 called 'Thrown Away'. It comes from their next album, about which no details of title or release date are yet available.

The tour, known as the 'Meninblack Tour', opens at Cardiff Top Rank on February 8 and continues at Bristol Locarno 9, Exeter University 10, Southampton Gaumont 11, Canterbury Odeon 12, Brighton Top Rank 13, London Hammersmith Odeon 15, Birmingham Odeon 16, Stoke Hanley Victoria Hall 17, Sheffield Polytechnic 18, Nottingham Rock City 19, Liverpool University 20, Manchester Apollo 21, Edinburgh Playhouse 24, Glasgow Apollo 25, Newcastle Mayfair 26, Lancaster University 27, Leeds University 28, Cleethorpes Winter Gardens March 2, Leicester De Montfort Hall 3.

Tickets are generally priced at £3.50 and £3.00, although Hammersmith is £4.00 and £3.50. Some box offices are open now and others won't have them until after Christmas, so you should check before going along to buy.

Rats pack

THE BOOMTOWN RATS have announced details of their British tour, which starts early in January and forms the first leg of a world trip. It will follow the release of their fourth album, 'Mondo Bongo', which was delayed after a dispute between the band and Phonogram International.

The album will now be released on December 26 — a peculiar release date to say the least!! It contains twelve tracks including a five-minute version of their single, 'Banana Republic', and a song called 'Under Their Thumb', with music by Jagger and Richards and words by the Rats.

The tour begins at Southampton Gaumont on January 4, followed by Bristol Colston Hall 5, Cardiff Sophia Gardens 6, Birmingham Odeon 7, Leicester De Montfort Hall 9, Manchester Apollo 10, Newcastle City Hall 11, Glasgow Apollo 13, Edinburgh Odeon 14, Sheffield City Hall 16, London Hammersmith Odeon 17.

Tickets are £3.50, £3.00 and £2.50 everywhere except Cardiff where they are all £3.50. They go on sale at the venues this Saturday.

Hazel goes nuts

HAZEL O'CONNOR, who completes her British tour this week coinciding with the release of her second album 'Sons And Lovers' on Albion, has lined up another batch of dates for January.

She'll be taking in places not covered by the first tour and starts at Glasgow Tiffany's on January 18, continuing at York University 20, Bradford St George's Hall 21, Oxford Polytechnic 23, Coventry Theatre 24, Bath Pavilion 25, Exeter University 26, Worthing Assembly Rooms 29.

Stranglers face frog march to prison

THE STRANGLERS got off to a grim start when they travelled down to Nice last week to defend themselves against charges of inciting a riot at Nice University during their much-publicised concert there in June.

The French prosecutor asked for a year's sentence for Jean Jacques Burnel for shouting at the crowd in French and six months for Jet Black and Hugh Cornwell because they only shouted in English. The judge will give his verdict next month.

Public bard

JOHN COOPER CLARKE, back from representing his country at the recent Poetry Olympics, has lined up a series of gigs before Christmas.

He appears at Sheffield Limit Club December 2, Edinburgh Playhouse 5, London The Venue 11, Liverpool Brady's 13, London Institute Of Contemporary Arts 15.

Buzz off

THE BUZZCOCKS have cancelled the second part of their 'occasional tour', which was due to begin this weekend. It's because of recording commitments and the band have expressed their disappointment. They hope to reschedule some of the dates around Christmas. Tickets can be refunded at the point of purchase.

BLONDIE on stage — a sight never to be repeated?

Blondie: the final curtain?

REPORTS that Blondie will never tour again were buzzing round the music business this week. Certainly the band, who've just released their new album on Chrysalis called 'Auto American', have no plans to play concerts anywhere at the moment.

Their last gigs were in fact in Britain at the beginning of this year. The dates were meant to be part of a world tour, but no other concerts materialised. Instead, the group went back to America and worked on the new album and various film projects. Debbie Harry has completed one film *Union City*, which should be screened here early next year, and also has cameo roles in Meatloaf's film *Roadie* and an upcoming edition of *The Muppet Show*. And another major film starring Debbie called *American Rhapsody* is in the pipeline.

Sources near to the band have stated that Blondie don't enjoy touring much and would prefer to get on with other projects for the time being. But they stress that this doesn't mean that the band won't ever play again — only that it may be some time.

Undertones tear up contract with Sire

THE UNDERTONES, who set out on their 'See No More' tour next week, have split from Sire Records after a number of 'irreconcilable' differences.

The band signed to Sire in September 1978 and have released two albums and seven singles. These will continue to be available to the end of March, when the rights will revert back to the group.

Quite what the 'irreconcilable differences' are hasn't been revealed, but the fact that the band have been able to leave the label and take all their material with them suggests that the contract they originally signed might not have been held to be legally binding in a court.

They are now considering "various methods of releasing future records", which could mean they will not be signing a normal record company contract. They intend to release a new single in January and say that they will be spending more time touring next year now that their contractual hassles are over.

They were hoping to play some additional Irish dates before Christmas, but these have now been postponed and a two-week Irish tour is being lined up for February.

Sire Records has just been acquired by Warner brothers, who have taken a 100 per cent interest in the company. Founder Seymour Stein will continue as president and as far as Britain is concerned it will continue to operate as a separate company. The label will concentrate on signing and promoting acts while Warner Brothers will handle all the 'non-creative' functions, such as pressing and distribution.

Police fix Xmas gigs

THE POLICE's on-off British Christmas dates are finally fixed after various licensing hassles were resolved at the weekend. They will now play two nights in a 5,000-capacity tent on London's Tooting Bec Common on December 21 and 22 and Stafford Bingley Hall 23.

All tickets are £5 as both venues will be unseated. The London tickets go on sale on Sunday, December 14 at Tooting Bec Common, London Theatre Bookings in Shaftesbury Avenue and Straight Music, 1-2 Munro Terrace, London SW10. The Stafford tickets will be on sale at the Bingley Hall and Mike Lloyd music shops, Coventry and Sheffield Virgin, Liverpool and Chester Perry Lane, Stafford Lotus, Wolverhampton Sundown, Birmingham Cyclops Sounds and Leicester Revolver. NO postal applications will be accepted.

These will be the only Police gigs in Britain for eight months and the proceeds will go to charity.

Anyone for Tea?

THE TEA SET (above), who released a single called 'Keep On Running' on Liberty Records recently, have lined up a series of support slots this month. They start by supporting Hazel O'Connor at London's Dominion theatre on December 5. They then play two dates with The Members at Crystal Palace Hotel 6 and Hammersmith Palais 8.

They then play with The Skids on their British dates at Exeter University 9, Keele University 11, Huddersfield Polytechnic 12, Leeds University 13, Oxford Polytechnic 14, Hull City Hall 16, Rickmansworth Waters Mete 17. They end with a gig of their own at Islington Hope And Anchor on the 29th.

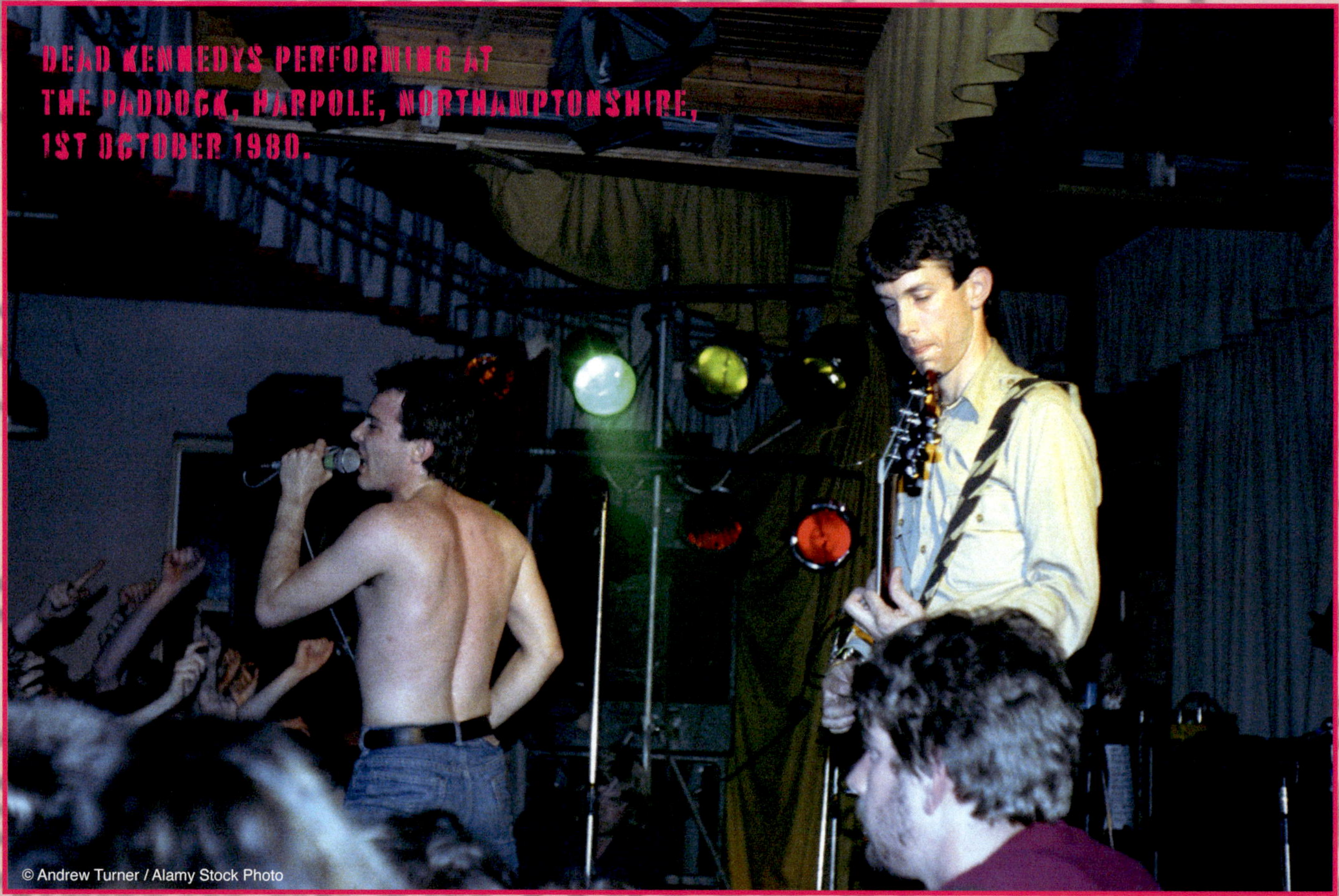

DEAD KENNEDYS PERFORMING AT THE PADDOCK, HARPOLE, NORTHAMPTONSHIRE, 1ST OCTOBER 1980.

DEAD KENNEDYS,
FROM LEFT: KLAUS FLOURIDE,
JELLO BIAFRA, D.H. PELIGRO,
EAST BAY RA.

© Steve Emberton

Old punks
TONIGHT the Doctors of Madness top the bill at the Mayfair, Newcastle. Rather belatedly, their record label are now trying to pass them off as one of the first punk bands.

THE AREA'S PREMIER NIGHTSPOT
20 CAROLGATE
RETFORD
Telephone 704981

PORTER HOUSE

OPEN 8.00 pm to 2.00 am — NO MEMBERSHIP REQUIRED
BASKET MEALS — DISCOUNT FOR PARTY BOOKINGS
ALL DRINKS 25p TILL 10.30 pm
NO ADMITTANCE UNDER 18 YEARS OF AGE

FRIDAY, 16th DECEMBER — 8.00 pm to 2.00 am

Don't miss the

Doctors of Madness
(UPSTAIRS)

PLUS DISCO ROADSHOW IN STEREO
(DOWNSTAIRS)

Admission: 95p 8 pm to 10 pm, 125p after 10 pm

THE CLASH, BIRMINGHAM, 1980.

Nick nick

CLASH drummer Nicky Headon was given a year's conditional discharge at London's Horseferry Road Magistrates Court last week when he admitted possessing quantities of cocaine and heroin.

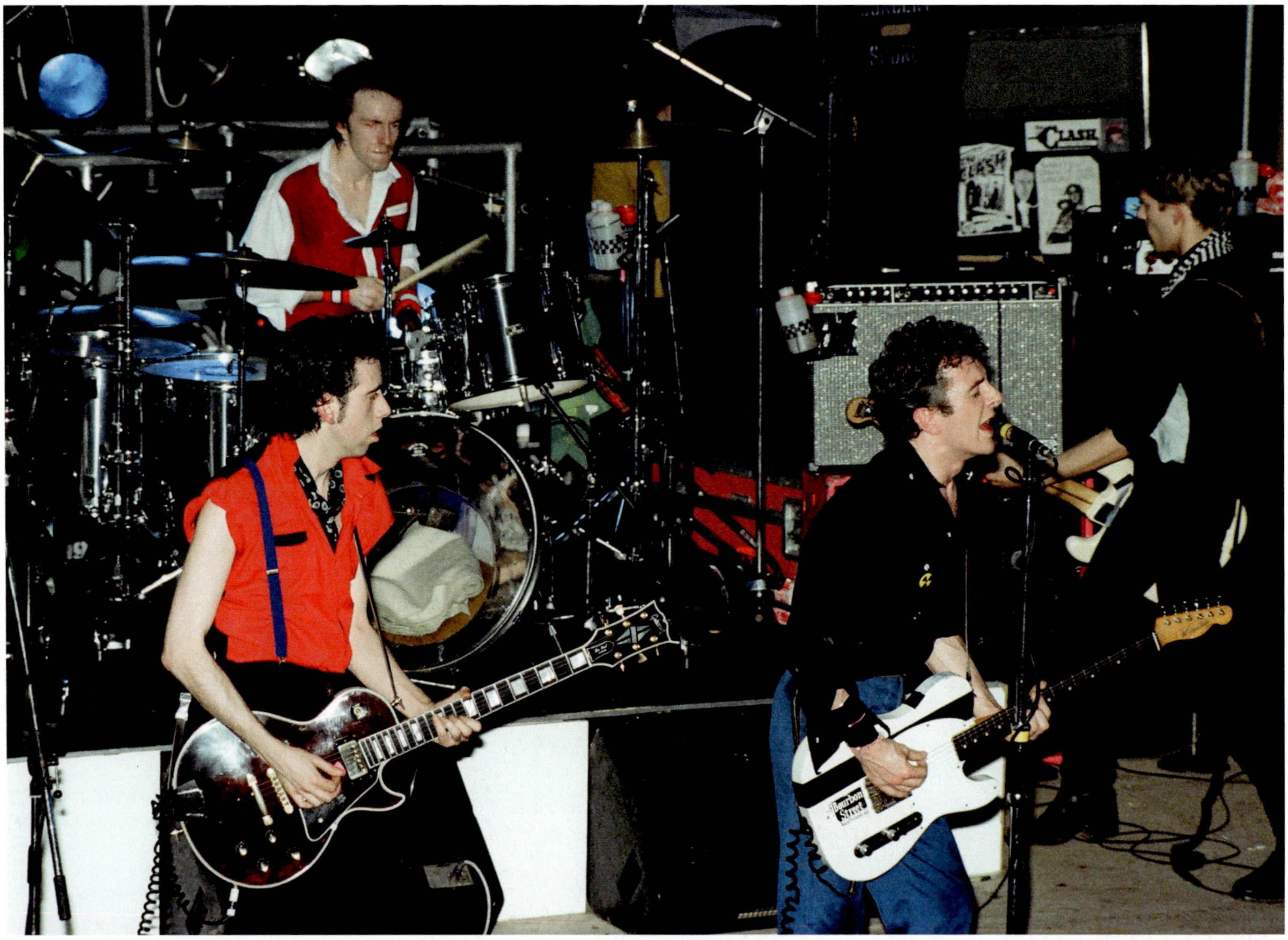
CLASH

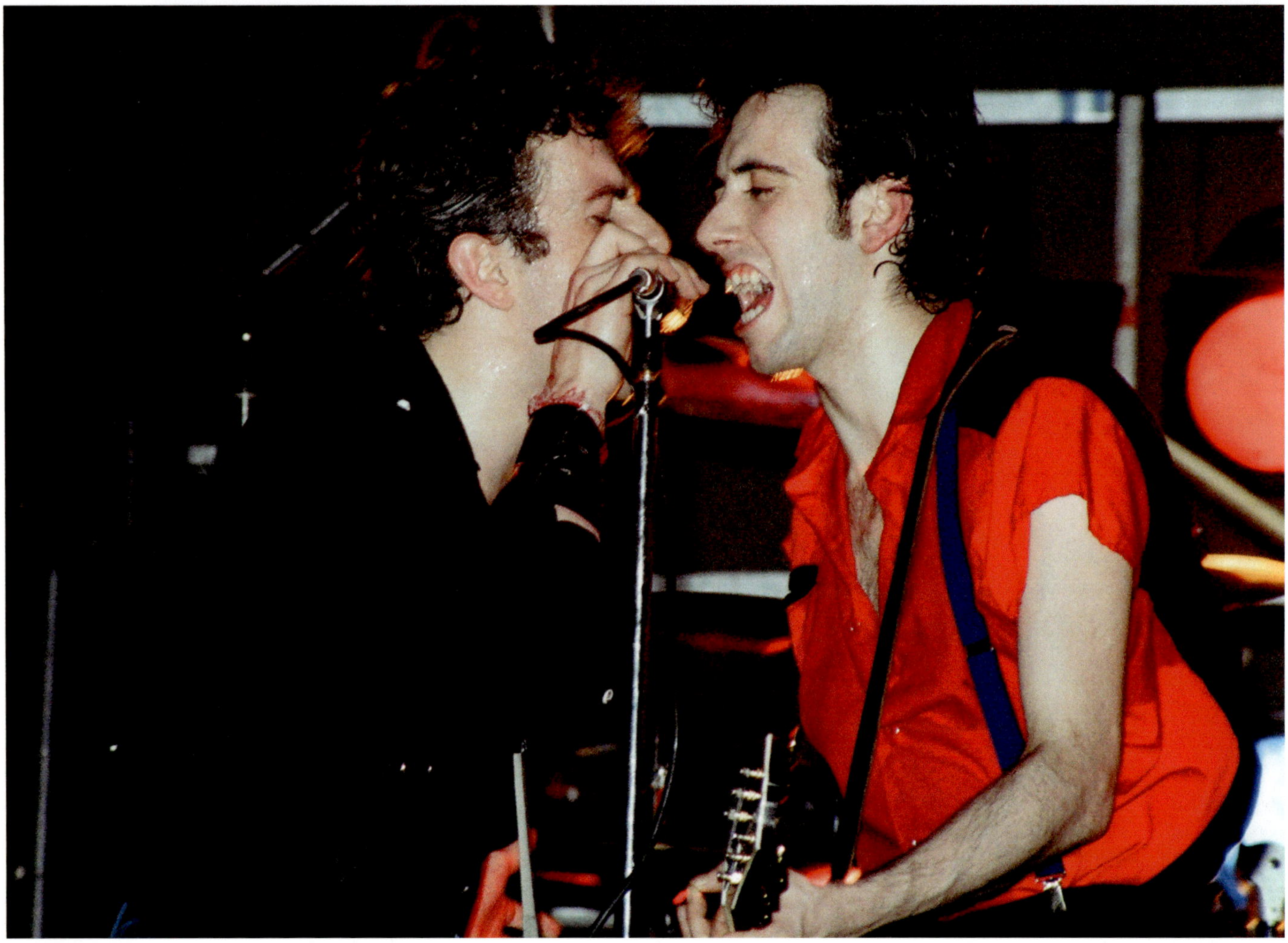

© Alan Perry

A RARE shot of Crass actually performing.

Crass megatour shock
(Well, three small benefit gigs actually)

CRASS have organised gigs over the Easter period to coincide with various peace marches and demonstrations around the country.

Together with Poison Girls, they play Bradford Queen's Hall on April 16 in aid of the END/CND trans-Pennine march, Witham Labour Hall 18 in aid of the CND Wethersfield Air Base demo and Birmingham Digbeth Civic Hall 22 in aid of Peace Centre and 021 Anarchists. All gigs will have a £1 admission and will be open to under-18s.

And those marching against nuclear bombs and cruise missiles around the country will find plenty of rock and roll to keep their feet moving. The Piranhas, The Mistakes and Between Pictures play at the demonstration at Greenham Common, Newbury, the proposed site for the cruise missiles, on April 20.

And The Beat play at a Peace And Music Festival in Rugy on April 20 organised by the West Midlands CND.

Derek Block in association with Dave Woods presents

Siouxsie and the Banshees
PLUS COMSAT ANGELS

Feb 16/17 HAMMERSMITH PALAIS 7.30 pm
All tickets £3.50 available from the Palais 01-748 2812 and usual agents.

Feb 19 POOLE ARTS CENTRE 7.30 pm
(Wessex Hall)
Tickets £3.50, £3.00 in advance from Box Office. (Poole) 85222

Feb 20th PORTSMOUTH GUILDHALL 7.30 pm
Tickets £3.50, £3.00 in advance from Box Office. 0705 24355

Feb 22nd DE MONFORT HALL, LEICESTER 7.30 pm
Tickets £3.50, £3.00 in advance from Box Office. 0533 54444

Feb 23 ASSEMBLY ROOMS, DERBY 7.30 pm
Tickets £3.50, £3.00 in advance from Box Office. 0332 31111

Feb 25th LEEDS UNIVERSITY S.U. 8 pm
All tickets £3.50. Available from Students Union. 0532 39071

Feb 27 EDINBURGH PLAYHOUSE 7.30 pm
Tickets £3.50, £3.00 in advance from Box Office. 031-557 2590

March 1 ROYAL COURT, LIVERPOOL 7.30 pm
Tickets £3.50, £3.00 in advance from Box Office. 051-708 7411

March 2 KING GEORGE'S HALL, BLACKBURN 7.30 pm
Tickets £3.50, £3.00 in advance from Box Office. 0254 58424 & usual agents.

March 3 NEWCASTLE CITY HALL 7.30 pm
Tickets £3.50, £3.00 in advance from Box Office. 0632 612606

SINGLE OUT NOW
ANTI-NOWHERE LEAGUE
DOUBLE-B-SIDE
STREETS OF LONDON + SO WHAT...
ON WXYZ RECORDS
ABCD 1
DISTRIBUTED BY FAULTY PRODUCTS & PINNACLE

Re-Member

THE MEMBERS have returned from a lengthy period of 'recuperation' following their dismissal from Virgin. In fact the band have been writing new songs and touring abroad.

They are back as a seven-piece with the original band plus horn players Steve 'Rudy' Thompson and Adam Maithland plus an 'occasional' percussionist when they feel like it.

They've signed a one-off deal with Albion and release a single called 'Working Girl' this week. They also have a series of gigs lined up at Liverpool Brady's May 16, Hammersmith Odeon (with XTC) 21, West Runton Pavilion 22, Retford Porterhouse 23, Birmingham Odeon 24 (with XTC), Rickmansworth Watersmeet 29, Canterbury Kent University June 7. More dates are being set up.

Jobson's break

RICHARD JOBSON, lead singer with The Skids and more recently, actor and poet, takes a short break from preparing for The New Skids first major British tour by undertaking a series of appearances at universities aimed at promoting 'The Ballad Of Etiquette', Richard's album of poetry.

It features Richard reading accompanies by musicians **Virginia** (flute/piano), **Josephine** (soprano sax, clarinet and piano) and **John McGeogh** (guitar).

Richard will be appearing at the venues detailed below with a similar line-up. 'The Ballad Of Etiquette' album is an aural version of Richard's recently published book of poetry, 'A Man For All Seasons'. The book contained Richard's own poetry, while 'The Ballad Of Etiquette' sees him reading the works of other poets.

Dates are: Uxbridge, Brunel University, October 19, Colchester, Essex University, 20, Reading, Reading University, 21, London, City University, 22, Middlesex Polytechnic, 23, (Two shows, lunchtime and evening); Norwich, East Anglia University, 24, Leicester, Leicester University, 26, Stoke-on-Trent, Keele University, 27, Nottingham University, 28, Durham, Durham University, 29, Newcastle, Newcastle University, 30.

Meanwhile, Richard, Russell Webb and the first new member of The Skids, Paul Wishart, are preparing a British tour aimed at supporting the release of their new album 'Joy', which is set for release on November 20.

Their new single, 'Iona'/'Blood And Soil' is released on November 11.

MCP presents
Stiff Little Fingers
with guests THE FLYING PADOVANIS
HAMMERSMITH PALAIS
THURS JAN 28th 8.00 p.m.
Tickets £3.50 available from Palais B/O, L.T.B., Albemarle, Premier B/O & Keith Prowse B/O's

Stranglers beat rap

THE STRANGLERS' court case in Nice, which followed the riot at their University gig there last spring, has now been concluded and all the band are safely outside prison walls.

Drummer Jet Black has written an account of what happened in a book called *Much Ado About Nuthing*, which will be published by the Stranglers Information Service next month. Details of how to get it will be announced later. Black himself describes the book as "a cynical view of a ridiculous situation."

The band are now rehearsing for their British 'Meninblack' tour, which starts next month. They've cancelled the Cardiff date on February 8, but added Durham University on the 23rd. A new single from the band called 'Thrown Away' is released next week, but there's no news of their next album as yet.

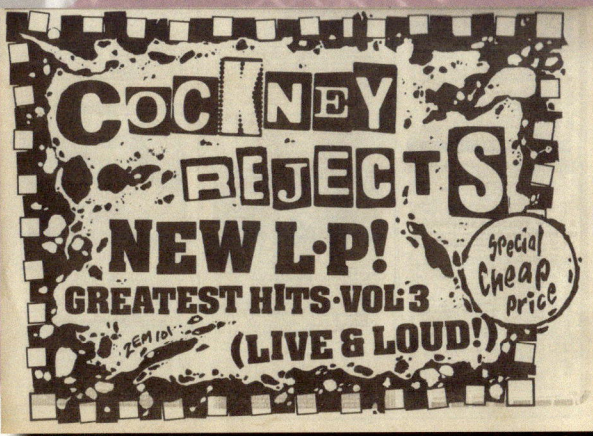

Out of a Rut

RUTS DC step out for their first British tour, since Malcolm Owen's death last summer, at the end of this month. And they have a new album called 'Animal Now' set for release on May 8 by Virgin.

The band, who are now back up to a four-piece with the addition of Gary Barnacle on saxaphone, start their tour at Manchester Polytechnic April 30, Birmingham Cedar Club May 1, Liverpool Royal Court 2, Edinburgh Nite Club 6, Middlesbrough Rock Garden 7, Scarborough Penthouse 8, West Runton Pavilion 9, Brighton Jenkinsons 10, Cheltenham Technical College 12, London Lyceum 14.

More dates will be added to this schedule in the next week or so.

Mrs Mills in a concrete overcoat

MICKEY GEGGUS, John Williams clone

Cockney Rejects/4-Skins/Erazerhead
Bridge House

500 WORDS to describe two of the best nights since VE Day — impossible unless I do it in stilted note book stylee. Sooo... Monday: house full signs up for the first time I can remember and even the walls are sweating.

Special guests the 4-Skins are up first, superb anarchic fun. That dodgy bass amp packing up must be part of the stage act, it relaxes everyone and allows Gary 'Mr Natural' Hodges to partake of some silly audience abuse.

Then it's manic pogo time down the front as the band power through a tasty ten stormers' worth of furious singalong cacophony. Hodges' sorethroat bark makes Jake Burns sound like Ella Fitzgerald and the ace newie 'Evil' shows the band are growing as writers at an alarming rate. It's a mighty drum-heavy high-velocity burst with tongue-in-cheek thug-rock lyrics and a great Ants style drum middle eight. The encore was inevitable with a re-run of 'Wonderful World' and 'Chaos'. Shambolic ecstacy all round.

Erazerhead support Tuesday, braving crowd indifference without a bassist. Slowly but surely they're licking the set into shape. Tonight it's ten Ramonesy vignettes instead of the old 18 and it works that much better for it. 'Get Pissed Again' to the tune of 'Let's Twist Again' has gotta be one of THE definitive r'n'r anthems...

The Rejects. How could I have doubted you? Monday was great but Tuesday was simply superb... and that's without such essential classics as 'Oi Oi Oi', and 'Sitting In A Cell With You'... Twelve numbers we got, and FOUR encores, and not even a bizarre police raid Tuesday ('Here They Come Again' — they found nothing wrong) could detract from the sense of occasion. They stand for so much, the East End's answer to the Pistols, in other words *the real thing*.

Listen to the lyrics of 'On The Waterfront', 'Police Car' and 'Hate Of The City' — to be quite honest it'd take a book to express it all (*Oh what a give-away — Ed*).

Their playing is tighter than your wildest dreams. Geggus' guitar exploding steel-cap hard, Stix's drumming pounding as heavy as Mrs Mills in a concrete overcoat, Vince's bass driving and confident, Stinky uglier and more self-assured than ever. They hit harder than John Conteh between courses, and, this is the BIG ONE, the new numbers worked really well live.

The mid-tempo almost Lizzyite 'Easy Life', the stompin' 'Cos I'm In Love' and the ultra-catchy 'Teenage Fantasy' were all well-received in the hand-clap and cheers stakes while a frenzied version of 'Motorhead' almost literally saw the dance floor cave-in.

But when you're talking about gen-u-ine 100 per cent uncontrolled euphoria it took 'War On The Terraces' 'Rip-Off', 'Fighting In The Street', and the aforementioned old classics (including 'Hate Of The City' with a tastefully drawn out guitar solo ending) to really hit the level of sheer unbridled WOARGHHNESS. And if you can imagine a 500-herbert-handed version of 'East End' with the Geggus hurling himself into the boiling hot billies...

I'm now more convinced than ever that the Rejects story is just beginning all over again. With legal hassles behind them, a red-hot set, and some real vinyl gems in the pipeline chartland oughta get itself prepared for a new Cockney invasion force. Just one thing though, tonight proved conclusively that refining their sound or not the Rejects are still pure Oi at heart. The First Wave Of Sophisticated Oi, maybe, but Oi none the less. You oughta stick with the rest of us, boys, together we can take on all the world...

GARRY BUSHELL

Wychfynde
Walsall

I'M NOT prejudiced against Heavy Metal, honest I'm not. Well not deliberately, anyway. I really did want to be nice about this band, if only to

HAZEL O'CONNOR, COVENTRY THEATRE, COVENTRY, 24TH JANUARY 1981

© Alan Perry

FEBRUARY 28 1981 30p

JU JU
Siouxsie, p17

Skins man

THE 4-SKINS have now been joined by former Cockney Rejects drummer **Nigel Wolfe**. He makes his first appearance with the band at a punk convention at Southgate Alan Pullinger Centre on January 9.

Stranglers

THE STRANGLERS release their new LP on November 9, entitled 'La Folie'. This will be the band's seventh album and is considered their most commercial for some time.

'La Folie' was recorded recently at the Manor. It was produced by the **Stranglers** and mixed by Tony Visconti.

A single, 'Let Me Introduce You To The Family', will be released on November 2.

The band's forthcoming tour dates are: Norwich, University, November 14, Birmingham, Odeon, 15, Cardiff, Sophia Gardens, 16, London, Hammersmith Palais, 17, Southampton, Gaumont, 19, Nottingham, Rock City, 20, Edinburgh, Playhouse, 22, Glasgow, Apollo, 23, Newcastle, City Hall, 24, Manchester, Apollo, 25, Liverpool, Royal Court Theatre, 26.

Jam dates

THE JAM have lined up four London dates in December. They'll play two nights at the Michael Sobell Sports Centre in Islington on December 12 and 13 followed by the Hammersmith Palais on the 14th and 15th.

Tickets are £4.50 and available by post only from MCP (to whom you should make cheques and postal orders payable to), PO Box 124, Walsall, West Midlands WS5 4AP. Allow at least a fortnight for processing and don't forget the sae.

The Jam's new single 'Absolute Beginners' is released by Polydor this week but there's no sign of an album to follow at the moment although one is certainly on the way.

Dickie dies after mystery shooting

CHUCK WAGON, (right) keyboards and sax player with The Dickies, is dead. Chuck shot himself at his parents' home in the Valley after getting back from a gig with the band. He died the next night in hospital, writes Silvie Simmons in Los Angeles.

The events leading up to the tragedy are still a bit blurred. Apparently Chuck was in an accident in which his car rolled over on the way back from the Dickies' Topanga Corral show at the weekend. He was driven home by the sound man. He went straight upstairs to his bedroom and shot himself in the head with a .22 caliber pistol.

Chuck — real name Bob Davis; the other name was given to him, along with his job, because he was the proud owner of a 1968 Volkswagen which he would use to transport various Dickies — had quit the band a few months ago and was working on his own material in New York. He came back to record the recently completed new Dickies album and to work the clubs with them after they came out of virtual retirement following A&M Records dropping them.

According to guitarist **Stan Lee**, the band's still in a state of shock and with no idea what their future will be. At least they're going ahead with the release of the album, a record they seem particularly pleased with.

Chuck Wagon's death is both sad and ironic. Among all the cynical, morbid L.A. punks, the Dickies always stood out as a band with a sense of silliness and humour.

The living Dead

THE DEAD KENNEDYS will visit Britain in October to play five dates at, as yet, unannounced venues.

While the band are over here they will be promoting the September re-release of their Cherry Red single 'Holidays In Cambodia', available on both 7" and 12". As usual it will be available through Rough Trade and Spartan Records.

Fresh Record Night
U.K. DECAY
MANUFACTURED ROMANCE,
BIG HAIR
at DINGWALLS on MONDAY FEB 16th
Admission £1.75

TOYAH WILLCOX, COVENTRY THEATRE, COVENTRY, 28TH JUNE 1982

A fanclub pack from Safari Records 1980.